Greatest Moments in
Tennessee
Vols Football History

Edited by Francis J. Fitzgerald

From the sports pages of

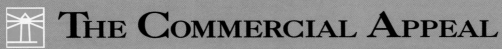

THE COMMERCIAL APPEAL

SP
SPORTS
PUBLISHING
INC.

THE COMMERCIAL APPEAL

Editor & President: Angus McEachran
Vice President & General Manager: Richard H. Remmert
Managing Editor: Henry A. Stokes
Deputy Managing Editor: Otis L. Sanford
Executive Sports Editor: John Stamm
Sports Columnist: Geoff Calkins
Deputy Sports Editor: Gary Robinson
Director of Photography: Larry Coyne
Director of Marketing: Elena Caiñas

ACKNOWLEDGEMENTS: Bud Ford, Haywood Harris, David Grim, Tom Mattingly and the staff at the University of Tennessee Athletics Media Relations Office, the FedEx Orange Bowl, the Nokia Sugar Bowl and AP/Wide World Photos, who assisted in providing key photos for this book. Also, a special thanks to Marvin West and Joe Welborn for their picks of the Vols' great games.

Robert Neyland: Gridiron General reprinted by permission of the estate of Tim Cohane.

ISBN 1-58261-019-3 (trade edition)

Produced by Epic Sports, Birmingham, Ala.
Cover Design by Chris Kozlowski, Boston, and Daniel J. Janke, Detroit.
Book Design by Daniel J. Janke, Detroit.
Photo Imaging by Philip Webb, Detroit.

Typefaces: Cheltenham, Minion, Giza.

Published in association with *The Commercial Appeal* by:

Sports Publishing Inc.
804 North Neil Street
Suite 100
Champaign, IL 61820
(217) 359-5940
http://www.sportspublishinginc.com

Introduction

Hey, it's not easy being sports editor in Memphis.

You needed to know that first off.

You see, we're located in Tennessee but ever so close to Mississippi and Arkansas. Pull out your map and check.

Then there's the matter of The Commercial Appeal circulating in all three states, reporting on such universities as Ole Miss, Mississippi State, Arkansas, Arkansas State and Vanderbilt. Then there's the large matter of the newspaper's base being in Memphis and home of the University of Memphis, and also having sizable pockets of SEC fans. And then there's the University of Tennessee being the state's largest university and having so many fans and so much success.

Finally, throw in the passion that football holds in these parts, and you've got a recipe that's hardly ready for the mixer: how does the newspaper provide enough coverage to satisfy all those fans and also serve the hometown university interest?

Yes, it's a never-ending balancing act worthy of the center ring.

So what do we do? We join in on the publishing of *Greatest Moments in Tennessee Vols Football History*. Yeah, I thought, that will make those other fans happy.

But my next thought was that's one book we'll have no trouble filling, what with all those magical Tennessee times, games, players and plays. Even those other schools' loyalists know UT football is big and worthy of chronicling. Just ask those Memphis fans how they felt after beating the Vols for the first time in 1996. Hey, did they ever find those goal posts?

Here it is then ... your history book about one of the country's tradition-rich, pride-thick football programs, as told in the pictures and stories by The Commercial Appeal.

Just what is Tennessee football?

It's moving Knoxville up the population charts with the filling of Neyland Stadium with 102,854 — that's capacity, usually more shoe-horn their way in — mostly bright-orange-dressed fans.

It's those 200 or so boats that cozy up to the banks of the Tennessee River near the stadium on game day for perhaps the nation's only floating tailgate party. The "Volunteer Navy" knows how to beat the traffic.

It's the players and coaches making the "Vol Walk" from Gibbs Hall to the stadium as the faithful line the walkway, calling out their praises and encouragement.

It's the "Pride of the Southland" marching band forming the giant "T" in the north end zone moments before kickoff, hitting the high notes in welcoming the Volunteer players, who are led by the blue tick coon hound named "Smokey." It's a tradition started in 1964 by former head coach Doug Dickey, the same year he put the "T" — orange, of course — on the helmets.

It's the incessant playing of *Rocky Top*, which debuted in 1972 and became gameday's most requested song in the mid-1970s. It's played after big plays and scores, which is often considering the Vols are known for their productivity. First-timers know it by heart by halftime.

It's Volunteer players running and diving into those checkerboard end zones — orange, of course — and a fixture since 1964.

It's Peyton Manning passing on the lure of the NFL and the big bucks so he would not be short-changed out of his senior season and all the joy he knew it would bring him.

It's winning.

It's tradition. As the Tennessee media guide says, "you know it when you feel it."

We believe you'll feel it with *Greatest Moments in Tennessee Vols Football History*.

It should suit you to a "T." Orange, of course.

John Stamm
Executive Sports Editor
The Commercial Appeal

Vols Score First Win Over Vandy

BY THE SPORTS STAFF
The Commercial Appeal

NASHVILLE, Nov. 7, 1914

For the first time in history, the University of Tennessee defeated Vanderbilt in football here today, 16-14.

It was simply a case of Vanderbilt being outplayed by the Volunteers. Tennessee scored her two touchdowns on forward passes — Bill May hitting Alonzo Carroll — for both scores and a field kick.

Both of Vanderbilt's touchdowns were made by Irby Curry, with the little quarterback going over once from the 1-yard line and again after a 20-yard run.

Vanderbilt's passing attack failed to complete a pass against the Vols' vaunted defense, which also grabbed three Vandy interceptions.

The Commodores' chief gains were around the ends, with Curry picking up most of the yardage.

When Tennessee had the ball, the Vols pounded their way through the Vandy line and used the pass at critical times.

Tennessee scored first, in the first quarter following three minutes of play. After driving downfield to Vandy's 30-yard line on the ground, May tossed a beautiful pass to Carroll in the end zone for a touchdown.

Carroll added the point-after kick to give the Vols a 7-0 lead.

Later in the first quarter, Carroll attempted a drop kick but it failed to make it over the goal posts.

Tennessee	7	6	3	0 –	16
Vanderbilt	0	7	0	7 –	14

Carroll was the star for Tennessee on this glorious afternoon, although May and Rus Lindsay, in the backfield, turned in a fine performance. Along with the two touchdown receptions, Carroll kicked the game-winning field goal in the third quarter.

In the second quarter, both teams scored a touchdown. Tennessee crossed the goal line first with a pass from May to Carroll. But Carroll missed the extra-point kick.

Trailing, 13-0, Vandy's Tom Lipscomb recovered a fumble on the Vols' 10-yard line. Fullback Glen Reams burst over tackle for five yards, Curry added two and Ammie Sikes raced around end for two yards to move the ball to the Vols' 1.

Curry then dove over the middle of the Vols' defensive line for the touchdown. Josh Cody added the Commodores' extra-point kick to narrow the Vols' lead to 13-7.

On the Vols' next series, the Vandy defense rallied and stopped Tennessee on three plays and then Cody blocked Farmer Kelly's punt, which was recovered by Martin Chester.

The first half ended moments later with Vandy at the Vols' 25.

In the third quarter, Lindsay led the Vols from its 25-yard line to Vandy's goal line, but the Commodores' defense held.

Vandy then punted to May at the Commodores' 30, who made a fair catch.

The Vols quickly struck, with Carroll booting his field goal to give the Vols a 16-7 lead.

When Vandy tried to rally by putting the ball in the air, May killed the Commodores' chances by making a key interception at Tennessee's 20-yard line.

Curry made Vanderbilt's final touchdown in the fourth quarter by darting through the entire Vol defense.

But it wasn't enough to overcome the Vols' 16-14 lead.

The Vols posted a record of 9-0 in 1914 and won the Southern Intercollegiate Athletic Association championship.

Vols Bury North Carolina

By The Associated Press
The Commercial Appeal

KNOXVILLE, Oct. 2, 1926

Tennessee started its Southern Conference campaign by swamping North Carolina today, 34-0.

The Tarheels gave less resistance than Carson-Newman did here a week ago and Coach Robert Neyland used his second-string players for most of the second half.

The game matched the Notre Dame and the Army systems, with the Vols grabbing all the glory. The Tar

| North Carolina | 0 | 0 | 0 | 0 – | 0 |
| Tennessee | 20 | 7 | 0 | 7 – | 34 |

Heel's coach, Chuck Collins — a Notre Dame grad, had instructed his men in the famed Notre Dame style of play, but it had not yet been mastered. Carolina was able to complete a few passes in the second half, but was unable to muster much of a ground attack the entire afternoon.

On the other hand, Vol coaches Neyland, Paul Parker and Bill Britton — all West point men — had trained their squad in a style of play which the Carolina players were helpless against.

The game had barely begun when Jimmy Elmore, the flashy little halfback, sprinted around end for 27 yards. A few plays later, Bill Harkness connected on an aerial to Charles Rice for a touchdown.

On the Vols' next series, Elmore & Co. marched downfield for a second touchdown. Elmore scored on a plunge over the middle.

Late in the first quarter, Elmore raced 30 yards around end for the Vols' third touchdown in one period. Afterward, Neyland began to send in his subs.

The Vols later added a touchdown in the second quarter and another in the fourth.

With North Carolina unable to test Tennessee, their real strength remains unknown. Fitted against an equal team, the Vols might rise to a style of play as yet not realized.

McEver Leads Vols to 15-13 Win Over Alabama

Tennessee	9	6	0	0	-	15
Alabama	6	0	7	0	-	13

BY THE ASSOCIATED PRESS
The Commercial Appeal

TUSCALOOSA, Ala., Oct. 20, 1928

An inspired Tennessee football team, led by two great sophomore halfbacks, Gene McEver and Buddy Hackman, today scored the greatest triumph in Volunteers' gridiron history by defeating Alabama, 15-13.

These youthful dynamos wrought havoc to Alabama's defensive tackles and ends all afternoon, slashing and twisting through them for decisive gains for victory.

Little Bill Hicks, big Tony Holm, Dave Brasfield and little John Henry Suther all gained great yardage for the Crimson Tide, ramming through the Vols' forward wall frequently for first downs, but when the opportunity presented itself to put the contest out of reach — and there were many — they either fumbled or found Tennessee tacklers blocking their path at every turn.

A homecoming crowd of 7,000, including several hundred Tennessee supporters and the Vols' band, saw one of the most thrilling games in recent Dixie football history.

Both Alabama and Tennessee scored within the first two minutes of play. McEver raced for 98 yards for a touchdown on the opening kickoff to give the Vols a 7-0 lead. Alabama then matched this total when Suther took the ball on a counter on the fourth play of the drive and darted 50 yards to reach the Vols' end zone.

It was the first time Tennessee and Alabama have played since 1914 and the first time the Crimson Tide has met disaster on its home field in modern football annals.

McEver, in returning the kickoff from his own 2-yard line, was never touched on his long jaunt to the Alabama goal. He raced the first half of his journey straight up the field, with Vols' blockers knocking down the Tide players. He then cut to the right side of the field behind two blockers, continuing within the sidelines by mere feet and sometimes inches, until he crossed the goal line.

The Tide came back with a vigorous drive through the line that could not be denied. Hicks ripped off a couple of first downs and Holm high-stepped over center for another. Then, at midfield, Suther slipped off tackle and cut to the right side of the field, outdistancing the sucked-in Tennessee secondary. After the Tide missed the point-after kick, Tennessee led, 7-6.

Near the end of the first quarter, Suther dropped back to his own goal to punt and Jess Eberdt, the Tide center, made a poor snap. The Vols' Harry Thayer quickly fell on the ball in the back of the end zone for a safety. This margin later proved to be the deciding points.

While leading, 9-6, the Vols exploded. Bobby Dodd, Amos Horner and McEver skirted around end to move deep into Alabama territory.

Then Dodd passed to Paul Hug at the Alabama 8.

The Vols attempted a pair of blasts up the middle and a pass, but to no avail. On fourth down, the Tide jumped off side and were penalized five yards down to the Tide 3.

Dodd again passed — and this time hit McEver, who scored the touchdown. Dodd's extra-point attempt was wide, but Tennessee was ahead, 15-6.

Vols Pass to Victory Against Vandy

By Blinkey Horn
The Commercial Appeal

NASHVILLE, Nov. 17, 1928

| Tennessee | 0 | 6 | 0 | 0 | – | 6 |
| Vanderbilt | 0 | 0 | 0 | 0 | – | 0 |

Gene McEver, a 1929 consensus All-American, set up the Vols' lone touchdown against Vandy.

Under skies that wept almost continuously from the kickoff to the final whistle, Tennessee vanquished Vanderbilt, 6-0, before a crowd of 22,000. It was the largest crowd to ever see a game in Tennessee.

The victory, which was the eighth scored this season by the Vols, gave the Orangemen its first win over a Vanderbilt team since 1916. It was also the second time in 24 games that the Commodores have been unable to score on the Vols.

Tennessee's victory leaves the Vols a perfect conference record and in a tie with Georgia Tech and Florida for the conference championship. The Vols play Florida in Knoxville on December 8.

The only touchdown in the game came in the second quarter. It was hatched from a 16-yard forward pass which Roy Witt, the defensive hero of the game, hurled to Paul Hug. The lone score was set up by a long punt return and an end sweep by Gene McEver that moved the ball down to the Vandy 7.

The next three plays the Vols lost nine yards. Then on fourth down, Witt flung a pass over the middle to Hug. He caught the ball at the Vandy 1-yard line and easily crossed the goal line.

Vanderbilt made two threats to score.

One came in the closing of the second period. The Commodores moved the ball from midfield after Johnny Askew replaced Paul McGaughy in the backfield. But Vandy was unable to score when Bill Schwartz' pass in the end zone went incomplete.

Then, with four minutes remaining in the game, the Commodores drove downfield from their 20. The drive was given additional life when Howell Warner caught a pass which had bounced from the grasp of several Tennessee players. But Vandy was

Bobby Dodd, Tennessee's quarterback magician, earned All-American honors in 1930.

unable to put the ball in the end zone.

Jimmy Armistead, who had been the leader of the Commodores' long march, had been injured prior to this series. Although he had lost his zip, he continued to pass. And Abner Abernathy, who had played magnificently during this contest, was unable to catch Armistead's final pass after it hit the tips of his fingers.

Armistead, who had been bottled up a week ago by Georgia Tech, came back with a vengeance against Tennessee. He nearly equaled the entire Vols' rushing total. Twice, he was alone in open field, with no one between him and the Tennessee goal line but Witt. Both times, the brilliant Vols leader hauled down the Vandy captain.

The Commodores made more yardage and first downs than Tennessee by a ratio of two to one. But the Vols managed to score the game's only touchdown.

Vandy's aerial game was blanketed by the Vols. They watched the Commodore receivers with hawklike alertness. Buddy Hackman, who hailed from Nashville, batted down pass after pass when it came within reach of a Vandy receiver.

And Arthur Tripp and Farmer Johnson turned in a splendid performance on the line for the Vols.

Vandy made repeated substitutions in their backfield in an effort to inspire a sustained touchdown drive. But the Vols' defense proved to be too stingy.

Brackett, Feathers & Volunteers Romp Over NYU

BY THE ASSOCIATED PRESS
The Commercial Appeal

NEW YORK, Dec. 5, 1931

Striking twice with dazzling swiftness in much the same spot, Tennessee's Volunteers came up from Dixie today to sweep New York University's rugged football forces off their feet and romped away with a 13-0 victory at Yankee Stadium in the first big game of the post-season metropolitan charity game series.

Favored by a clear, crisp afternoon, the game attracted 40,684 spectators who contributed $70,597 in gate receipts — the bulk of which, after expenses are deducted, will go to benefit the unemployed of New York City and Knoxville, the hometown of the Volunteers.

The crowd, filling about half of the big American League ballpark, was rewarded for its turnout by watching one of the finest intersectional games of the year. Tennessee's victory kept the team's unbeaten record intact for the 1931 season and marked the end of the glorious career of Gene McEver, the famous Vols halfback, who earned the distinction of never having tasted defeat in a varsity game.

It was New York's third setback at the hands of an intersectional rival, and the most decisive, suffered by the Violets this season.

While the violet-clad players were busily engaged watching and waiting for the celebrated McEver to start going places with the ball, two of his teammates — Beattie Feathers and Deke Brackett — put on an exhibition of broken-field running that sewed up the game tighter than a bale of cotton.

Both Tennessee touchdowns came within five minutes of each other, and brought the big crowd to its feet in thrilling acclaim. Feathers, on a surprising jaunt, raced 65 yards for the Vols' first score after it appeared he had been stopped, only to break away from his tacklers and get into the clear.

Shortly afterward, Brackett, the Vols' substitute quarterback, plucked one of NYU tailback Jim Tanguay's high spirals out of the air on the Vols' 26, then slowly picked his way to one side of the field, zig-zagged toward the other sideline, and completed a 74-yard scoring dash with the aid of superb blocking assistance.

At least a half-dozen New York players had a chance to bring Brackett down in his downfield sprint, but none could keep a firm grasp on this elusive Vol back.

Tennessee	0	13	0	0	– 13
NYU	0	0	0	0	– 0

Deke Brackett's 74-yard pass reception from Jim Tanguay for a touchdown sealed the Vols' win over NYU in the Charity Classic.

McEver dove over the middle for the first point-after but failed in his attempt to kick the second one. The remainder of the afternoon, the veteran Tennessee backfield ace was devoted to blocking, passing, making defensive tackles in the secondary and occasionally carrying the ball, but mostly he served as a decoy. McEver's longest gain from scrimmage was 16 yards as he yielded the spotlight of all-around performance to Feathers, whose brilliant kicking and running played a big part in the Vols' victory.

Not only was New York's defensive play below standard, especially in the line, but the Violets showed a complete lack of scoring punch in the two chances they had to push over a touchdown. The Violet line were outplayed by the southerners, who were led by Herman Hickman, the 218-pound right guard.

Hickman, a reminder of Yale's famous Cupid Black, swarmed all over the Violets and plucked them on all sides of the line of scrimmage and made half of the Vols' tackles on defense.

Late in the first quarter, Tanguay connected on a 42-yard pass to Charles Hugret to put NYU on the Vols' 8-

yard line after two earlier threats by the Vols had been turned back.

This gave the southerners their first chance to display their defensive stuff and they rose to the emergency by taking the ball on downs as Joe Lamark's last lunge for a touchdown failed by a matter of inches. It took the officials several moments to decide whether Lamark had crossed the goal line or not and the Violet rooters booed the adverse decision lustily.

After being swept off their feet and outclassed in the second period, when the Vols rushed and passed for a total of 237 yards, NYU rallied with another passing attack in the third quarter. Two long Violet passes, with Hugret on the receiving end of the second pass, put the ball on the Vols' 5-yard line. Here the Vols exhibited the defensive stand of the game. They not only stopped four straight Violet dives into the line, but set their rivals back five yards in the bargain, taking the ball on downs on the 10-yard line.

From there, Tennessee's defense was airtight against all of NYU's threats, through the air or the line, and the Vols had no trouble preserving their decisive margin.

This contest was Tennessee's first invasion of the north in eight years and Maj. Bob Neyland's pupils celebrated with another fine contribution to their long string of victories. It was their fifty-second victory in six years against only two defeats and four ties. The only time they were checked this season was by Kentucky in a 6-6 tie.

Tennessee converted nine first downs to NYU's eight and rushed for 225 yards to the Violets' 56. In the air, the Vols only completed one pass for 13 yards while NYU completed seven passes for 148 yards.

Tennessee Rallies to Defeat Crimson Tide, 7-3

| Tennessee | 0 | 0 | 0 | 7 | – | 7 |
| Alabama | 0 | 3 | 0 | 0 | – | 3 |

BY THE ASSOCIATED PRESS
The Commercial Appeal

BIRMINGHAM, Oct. 15, 1932

In a fiercely fought battle, always centered around a punting duel between Tennessee's Beattie Feathers and Alabama's John Cain, the Vols capitalized on a fourth-quarter break in rain-drenched Legion Field today to eliminate the Crimson Tide from the Southern Conference football championship race, 7-3.

The Tide scored their field goal in the second quarter after a march from midfield had been stopped on the Vols' 4. Hillman Holley arched the ball squarely between the goal posts from the 12-yard line to put the Tide ahead, 3-0. This slender lead looked good until the fourth period when Feathers, the vaunted Vols halfback, punted the ball dead on Alabama's 1-yard line. Here was the break the Vols had been waiting for, and they were quick to take advantage of it.

Standing behind his goal line, Cain fumbled a bad snap from center and attempted to kick, with a group of orange-clad players swarming in on him. He sliced the kick out to the 11-yard line. A few minutes later, Feathers shot around left end for a touchdown. Herman Wynn added the point-after kick to give the Vols a 7-3 lead.

Cain perhaps was guilty of an error in judgement in this close spot, but he chose to kick rather than accept a safety which would have given his team a one-point lead and might have resulted in victory.

The kicking duel was almost over between Feathers and Cain, with Cain probably having a slight edge in distance. Punts of 60 and 70 yards were common, even with the wet and slippery ball, which was hard to catch and equally hard to kick cleanly. Cain's average for the game was slightly less than 50 yards, while Feathers was only a few yards shy of this average.

More than 20,000 spectators sat huddled in the concrete stands as the cold wind and rain swept past and peered down through the mist on this contest which meant glory or oblivion for the mud-spattered teams.

The Notre Dame offensive system, featured by Alabama, was virtually voided by the soggy field, while Tennessee's running plays — also built around the speed in the winged feet of young Feathers — were of little value. Tennessee's victory marked the second time in as many years that the Volunteers had shattered Alabama's title aspirations.

Murray Warmath

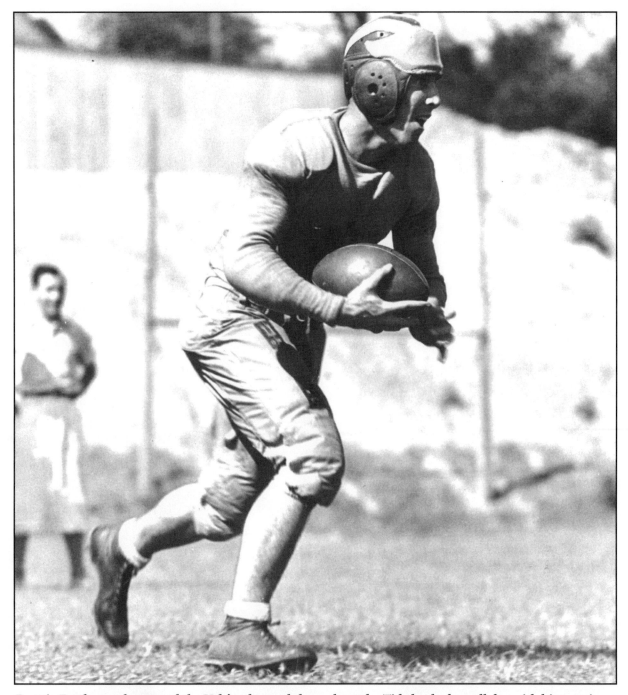

Beattie Feathers, who scored the Vols' only touchdown, kept the Tide backed up all day with his punting.

Feathers, a 175-pound halfback from Bristol, Va., brought the Vols' rooters to their feet in the opening period as he cut loose from midfield on a 37-yard run to the Alabama 14.

An intercepted pass halted this drive and the teams settled back to their plan of punting and waiting for the breaks.

The Volunteer line rose up in all of its might in the second quarter to thrust back Alabama's first bid after Newton Godfree, an Alabama tackle, had recovered a Vols' fumble by Richard Dorsey on the Tennessee 16-yard line.

Alabama's runners were then tossed for a net loss of eight yards in four tries.

Tennessee Trounces Oklahoma in Orange Bowl

BY WALTER STEWART
The Commercial Appeal

MIAMI, Jan. 1, 1939

Buist Warren sweeps right against the Sooners. The Vols outrushed Oklahoma, 232 yards to 97.

Sluggish as a sleep-shackled grizzly crawling into the Spring sun with wicked red eyes half-closed against the glare, the Tennessee Vols lashed out spasmodically here today and deflected the blows landed squarely upon its delicate flesh by the Sooners of Oklahoma.

When the last broken bone was whipped back into place, when the last eye had retreated into mourning, some statistician took a fugitive gander at the scoreboard and announced that Tennessee had won, 17-0. It wasn't a very good game, if you must insist on the truth, but it was so utterly ferocious that women fainted and strong men turned away their faces — pale faces, too.

This contest matched the Indians of Oklahoma and Tennessee's mountain men and the mountain men were able to shoot a bit faster — and with more accuracy.

Midway through the first quarter, Tennessee wingback Bob Foxx knifed through Sooner grasps for eight yards and a touchdown. Bowden Wyatt's point-after kick was blocked, but the brilliant Vols back outraced several Sooners to the ball, picked it up and dashed to the goal line for the extra point to give Tennessee a 7-0 lead.

The Vols' second quarter scoring was set up when the small, but durable Bob Andridge collared Sooner

Oklahoma	0	0	0	0 —	0
Tennessee	7	3	0	7 —	17

Bob Seymour's fumble on the Oklahoma 27. Four plays later, Wyatt booted a field goal from the 24 and the crowd of 32,191 in the Orange Bowl screamed wildly as the Vols led, 10-0.

In the fourth quarter, Babe Wood later rattled 19 yards for the Vols' final touchdown, which completed a 73-yard drive from the Tennessee 27. Wood's spectacular run went from one side of the field to the other as he headed straight for the goal line corner. He hit it as he scored — less than a yard inside the sideline. Afterward, the Sooner players carried him over to the grandstand and gave him a free seat. Foxx's extra-point kick gave the Vols a comfortable 17-0 lead and the eventual win.

The play on the field was so fierce that Oklahoma the Sooners gained a total of 97 yards rushing and passing and lost 90 yards in penalties. The Sooners might have lost more in penalty yards if the officials had stopped looking at the sky long enough to observe more of the game.

Tennessee gained 232 yards and lost 130 yards on penalties.

A pair of Sooner defenders were unable to stop this pass deep in OU territory.

Babe Woods' TD run was the play of the game.

Prior to the game, Vols coach Bob Neyland had noted that his squad "had come just for the trip, was not mentally in the game and were going to play bush-league football."

Well, Maj. Neyland was wrong about the team playing bush-league football because the Volunteers played hard and bravely. They blocked explosively, but did not show the offensive might which had taken them to the top of the college football world.

It may not have been the Vols' best day, but it definitely wasn't a Sooner day.

Alabama	0	0	0	0 –	0
Tennessee	0	7	0	14 –	21

Butler Leads Vols to 17th Straight Victory

BY WALTER STEWART
The Commercial Appeal

KNOXVILLE, Oct, 21, 1939

In This Corner . . . By Art Krenz
IT'S ALL UP TO HIM, NOW

BOB FOXX
TENNESSEE'S TOP SCORER ..

FOXX' PET SCORING PLAY

— WITH TAILBACKS GEORGE CAFEGO AND JOHNNY BUTLER SLOWED DOWN BY KNEE INJURIES BOWL-BOUND VOLS MUST DEPEND ON FOXX FOR MAJOR PART OF OFFENSIVE DUTIES... THIS 180-POUND JUNIOR IS CONSIDERED SMARTEST AND MOST VERSATILE ATHLETE IN TENNESSEE HISTORY ....
KRENZ

Striking with a spearhead fire, new from the freshman furnace, the University of Tennessee today impaled Alabama's Red Elephant and left him wallowing in 21-0 misery.

Of course there were three touchdowns, but only one made much difference and this was scored by a weasel-hipped sophomore named Johnny Butler — a 160-pound hobgoblin who haunted Alabama over 56 yards which should be strung together and hung among the highest spikes in the Volunteer Trophy Room. It wasn't just a run with a football. It was physical effort raised to the level of epic poetry — a display of glory which gripped 40,000 and stopped one of them forever.

As little Butler whirled out of the last pair of Crimson arms, Alvis Wade rose from his seat in the high packed stands and fell forward on his face and died. Death comes to all of us and when it comes to me I hope that it will be as gay and debonair — with the pulsing thunder of a great cheer rolling down the slopes of the stadium — with keen October nipping at the flanks of summer with a halfback like Butler raging through the last five yards.

For Butler was a man inspired as he cut over his left tackle and squared away for the right sideline. He turned with the turf spurting from beneath his cleats and came back — came back alone — a wisp of Orange in a brutal wave of Red. For his blockers had been swept away in that first burst. He veered toward the left with tacklers roaring on his slim flanks.

Again they penned him up — slashing at the bobbing helmet. Then he whirled again — and found 240-pound Fred Davis reaching for him — a great bear of a man with hands like tree branches. Here Butler got his only solid block, hesitated for a moment while some anonymous hero cut big Davis down, then he charged the last white line,

Johnny Butler (22) rips for 56 yards en route to the Alabama goal line.

leaving the Alabama players well behind him.

After that it was a matter of massive thrusts and passes as a desperate Crimson eleven tried to regain the momentum.

Just before Butler pinned them down, Alabama had rambled to the Tennessee 29 with the aid of a 15-yard roughing penalty. But was stopped as the Tennessee line rose in defense. Sandy Sanford — the Crimson end whose toe had turned so many forlorn hopes into victory — then stepped to the firing tee.

The ball was placed down on the 37 but Tennessee smashed through and Sanford scraped the ground with his erring cleats and the ball barely reached the goal line. He never had another chance.

Butler worked his elfin magic and his Volunteer teammates played crashing football to turn two

fourth-period Alabama drives into touchdowns.

Paul Spencer fumbled on his own 11 deep in the final quarter and ponderous Joe Wallen recovered it for Tennessee. Then Butler slipped the ball back to Bob Foxx who skirted his left end, bounced from the sidelines and plunged over for the touchdown.

With a minute to go, this raiding Foxx intercepted one of Charley Boswell's frantic passes and took it to the Alabama 12. This time, Buist Warren was in the tailback station and the reverse was called again. But

Warren held the ball concealed behind him as the Elephants rushed yelling at the speeding Foxx — Warren then ran through left tackle and reached the end zone without being touched.

But you must always come back to Butler's swirling challenge.

"It was the greatest run I've seen since Grange," said Francis Wallace in the press box. Wallace is a magazine sports writer for *The Saturday Evening Post* who knows almost all there is to know about football.

Vols Tame Auburn to Win 23rd Straight

By Walter Stewart
The Commercial Appeal

Knoxville, Dec. 9, 1939

Auburn	0	0	0	0	–	0
Tennessee	0	7	0	0	–	7

S wift as golden falcons sweeping down the wind, the men of Tennessee descended upon Auburn's ramparts and burst them with one spear-bristling sortie.

After winning, 7-0, the Vols scaled the final peak and looked down upon the promised land of Southern California. Far torn banners of Orange and White streamed above them, banners stiff with honor. It was Tennessee's 23rd straight win and the 15th consecutive game in which the Vols had kept another team out of its end zone.

Auburn fought with solid fury this afternoon and lashed out at the Tennessee defense with an iron scourge and battered the Vols backs, sending them reeling on their heels.

But little Johnny Butler played for Tennessee today — and he made all the difference.

Early in the second quarter, Butler dropped back to pass, ducked beneath the defensive rush and turned upfield on a 40-yard touchdown rush which choked the breath of 20,000 and then spilled it out in a wild cry which shook the echoes over Pasadena. He looped left end, cut through two pairs of clawing ends and

bounced from his left sideline. Butler then whipped back into the open, where Auburn's Lloyd Cheatham nailed him hard, clamping his arms around the thrashing legs, but Butler spun and sent Cheatham sprawling. A group of Tennessee players soon joined him and provided an escort to the goal line. Ike Peel's point-after kick gave the Vols a 7-0 lead — and the winning total.

Tennessee's march to the Auburn end zone covered 65 yards in four plays. For the rest of the afternoon, the Vols attempted the harsh business of protecting their lead.

For one bruising quarter — the second quarter this afternoon against Auburn — the Vols played like the Tennessee team of 1938, who used to earn its touchdowns by long marches up the opposing team's spines. Butler's long run notched the end zone a few minutes later when the Orange legion roared 82 yards to the Auburn 5 only to be stopped when a pair of passes fell incomplete.

But Tennessee had the iron fibred quality which is fused into every great team — the ability to tap the reserve tanks when fuel is most needed. It was just enough to carry them through the tough times to victory.

Maj. Robert Neyland's clan, however, got no breaks today. Auburn got the key fumbles and interceptions. Yet when the battle crossed into Vols' territory, the challenge was met with muscle bunched along the jawline and feet planted in the bedrock.

Auburn's most serious raid reached the Tennessee 29 and there it was smashed by an Orange calvary.

The Vol team during a visit to the Rose Bowl prior to their game against Southern Cal.

Mighty Trojans Humble Vols in Rose Bowl

By WALTER STEWART
The Commercial Appeal

Pasadena, Calif., Jan. 1, 1940

Tennessee's buckskin eleven fell back before the mighty walls of Troy today, shattered themselves in futile rushes which fell far short and then limped away into the night carrying the short end of a 14-0 score. But they carried it in grubby paws smelling of heroism.

There was once another Troy and a woman named Helen and a warrior band which came to raid the countryside. Today, there was no Archilles with his sword of thunder, no ranging Ajax and no godlike Hector. But the war fought out in the gulch of Arroyo Seco would have brought fresh fame to the Troy of a long time ago.

The ancient stratagem of the wooden horse would not work today and Tennessee had no guileful Ulysses to spring the trap. They fought with all the brawn and courage that nature had given them and it was simply not enough.

Outmanned and overpowered by a Southern California team which rolled on juggernaut wheels, they battled to that final bridge and fell into its depths below with their tattered orange banner still flogging in the wind.

Tennessee	0	0	0	0	– 0
USC	0	7	0	7	– 14

A crowd of 90,000-plus packed the Rose Bowl to view the USC-Tennessee game.

The 14-0 defeat in the Rose Bowl, which was witnessed by a crowd of more than 90,000, shattered two records that the Vols had been building for nearly two seasons. When USC's Ambry Schindler crossed the goal line in the second quarter, he halted a 15-game streak in which the Vols had not allowed their opponent to score against them — a streak which began in the 1938 season when LSU's Ken Kavanaugh caught a pass in the end zone. USC also halted a 23-game Vols' winning streak.

Tennessee was utterly outplayed in the Rose Bowl. They were pushed from one end of the field to the other. Today, the football gods and the biggest guns were on the side of Southern California.

Outrushed 253 yards to 91, outweighed and driven before the bitter storm of Trojan backs, Tennessee might have snatched a hard victory if there had been an even shake in the breaks.

USC's first touchdown came with less than a minute in the first half. Behind Schindler's superb ball carrying, USC stormed from the Vols' 47 to the 21. The Trojans fury was directed between the ends. Schindler then romped to the Vols' 6. A roughing penalty against Tennessee then moved the ball to the Vols' 1. Two plays later, Schindler dove over for the touchdown. Bob Jones' point-after kick gave USC a 7-0 lead.

The Vols may have been able to defense Trojan backs

All-American halfback George Cafego's knee injury forced him to the sideline after the first quarter.

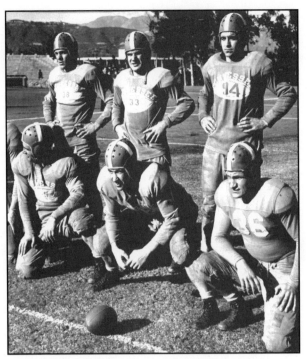

The 14-0 loss to Southern Cal ended the Vols' 23-game win streak.

Grenny Lansdell and Doyle Nave, but they could not stop Schindler. He beat the Vols into submission. It was the worst defeat of a Neyland-coached Tennessee team had suffered since 1926, when his Volunteers were hammered by Vanderbilt, 20-3.

Tennessee's greatest moment came midway in the third period. With the ball on the Vols' 1-yard line, little Johnny Butler stepped into his end zone to punt on first down. Instead, he passed to Emil Hust, who was dragged down at the Vols' 18. Joe Wallen, Butler and Fred Newman took turns in moving the ball to the Vols' 36.

As the fourth quarter began, Bob Foxx got the ball on a reverse and passed to Jimmy Coleman at the USC 38. Coleman then caught another pass at the Vols' 27.

On another reverse, Foxx tossed a pass to Ed Cifers for 7 yards. Warren added 2 yards to move the ball to the USC 18. However, Newman's fumble on the next play halted the drive. It would be the closest Tennessee ever got to the USC end zone.

The consensus among the sportswriters covering the game was that George Cafego was the Tennessee team. Cafego played almost a full quarter today, but he was not the Cafego of the LSU and Alabama games. He could not cut back on his aching knee or drive with his fabulous power. Cafego was not up to par and Tennessee sagged with him.

USC's final score came soon after Tennessee's unsuccessful drive deep into Trojan territory. Schindler and Jack Banta combined to lead the Trojans from the USC 18 to the Vols' 26 in seven plays. Schindler then passed to Roy Engle for 4 yards and Banta hit the middle of the Vols' defense on two straight plays to take the Trojans to the Vols' 7. Schindler added 4 yards to the Vols' 3.

On fourth down, Al Krueger caught a lob pass in the end zone. Phil Gasper's point-after kick gave USC a 14-0 lead which was enough to eventually win the contest.

For Tennessee fans, it was a long afternoon watching their team ripped apart and overpowered.

The 1940 Volunteers were named National Champions with a record of 10-1.

Warren Leads Vols' Comeback Against Alabama

Tennessee	0	14	0	13	–	27
Alabama	0	6	6	0	–	12

BY WALTER STEWART
The Commercial Appeal

BIRMINGHAM, Oct. 19, 1940

Lashed forward by a demoniac little man with stormy eyes, Tennessee broke out of Crimson shackles this Butler-crested Saturday afternoon and struck Alabama blind with a pair of iron-bound blows and plunged massively on a 27-12 triumph in front of 24,531 at Legion Field.

The Orange bruisers' attack almost fell apart in the second quarter when Alabama's Jimmy Nelson ripped for 14 yards to the Vols' end zone. But three plays later, Maj. Robert Neyland's troops were pouring over the Alabama goal line to even the score at 6-6. Afterward, their throathold never slackened.

Johnny Butler was Tennessee's spark plug today. Butler ran out of the shadow cast by Alabama's first touchdown. Taking over after the kickoff at the Vols' 21, Butler swept around end and raced to the Tide 11 for a 68-yard gain. On the next play, he passed to Al

Johnny Butler passed for one touchdown and ran 49 yards for a second touchdown.

Hust for a touchdown. Fred Newman's extra-point kick gave the Vols a 7-6 lead.

Eight plays later, Butler fielded Alabama's punt at the Tide 49 and ghosted his way through the swarming red-shirted Alabama players who were in pursuit of him for the Vols' second touchdown. Newman's point-after kick increased the Vols lead to 14-6.

In the third quarter, Alabama's Brown got the chance to pay back Butler and Tennessee. Fielding Butler's punt at the Tide 43, Brown followed his blocking, ran through a half-dozen Vols players and into the end zone to narrow the score to 14-12. Charley Deshane missed the point-after kick.

On their next series, Alabama missed a 38-yard field goal which Buist Warren returned to the Vols' 33. That was practically the end of Alabama, but Neyland's squad was just catching its second breath.

After advancing the ball to the Alabama 40, Warren ran and passed the Vols for 33 yards over the next nine plays. On fourth down, Warren chucked the ball to Mike Balitisaris who cut sharply to the right and made his catch in the end zone. Newman's extra point pushed the Vols lead to 21-12.

A few plays later, a poor Alabama punt set up Tennessee at the Tide 26. Two runs and a pass failed to produce a first down, so on fourth down Warren fired a pass to Balitisaris at the Tide 6. On the next play, he ran the remaining distance for his second touchdown of the afternoon. Unfortunately, Newman's extra-point kick was wide.

Still, the Vols' 27-12 lead was too much for Alabama to catch up to.

Tennessee's great line: (left to right) Coleman, Shires, Molinski, Ackerman, Suffridge, Luttrell and Cifers.

Tennessee Vanquishes Tough Tulsa, 14-7

BY DAVID BLOOM
The Commercial Appeal

NEW ORLEANS, Jan. 1, 1943

Dauntless determination carried Tennessee to a 14-7 Sugar Bowl victory over Tulsa today.

Set back seven points by the most amazing passing demonstration in college football history and badgered by incredibly bad luck — including bring cheated of a touchdown, this valorous Volunteer team stuck steadily to its guns to wipe out the memory of a Boston College defeat here two years ago and to even up its bowl score at two won and two lost.

Tennessee, however, will never forget a long, talented young man named Glenn Dobbs — and neither will the 70,000-plus in Sugar Bowl Stadium. Throwing with unbelievable accuracy, this Oklahoma back completed seven straight passes that carried Tulsa 60 yards down the field to a touchdown on the first play of the second quarter.

The Sugar Bowl has showcased the talents of great quarterbacks such as Davey O'Brien and Sammy Baugh, but New Orleans fans have never seen a passer like Dobbs. He threw to Saxon Judd, to Cal Purdin and to John Greene just as if he was spotting that ball on a dime, leaving Tennessee

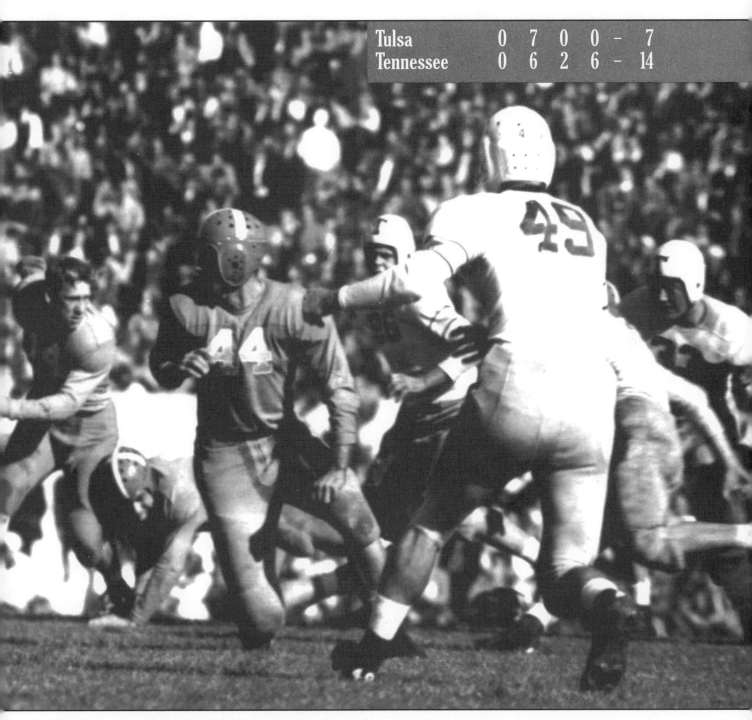

Tulsa	0	7	0	0	-	7
Tennessee	0	6	2	6	-	14

Tennessee outrushed the Golden Hurricane, 296 yards to 39.

players and the Sugar Bowl crowd with their mouths open. And he added this to a punting lesson that almost matched the aerial performance.

Fortunately, Tennessee only had to contend with this passing barrage in the first half and only 10 minutes of the last two periods.

The Vols were clearly the better team. They passed their way to set up a second quarter touchdown, with Bill Gold ramming it in for the touchdown. Charlie Mitchell, however, missed the point-after kick which left the Vols behind, 7-6.

Later in the third quarter, Tennessee went up, 8-7,

Tennessee had ever scored in the Sugar Bowl.

Although one Dobbs toss was as good as another, it was the one to Purdin that paid off in Tulsa's only touchdown, in the second quarter. Clyde LaForce added the extra-point that briefly give Tulsa the lead, 7-0.

Late in the fourth quarter, N.A. Keithly almost got Tulsa back in the game following a fumble by Walter Slater near midfield with less than two minutes left to play. Judd caught a pass for 14 yards that moved the ball into Tennessee territory. Keithly then passed to Green, who grabbed the pass between two Vols defenders at the Tennessee 30. After several passes fell incomplete, Green leaped high to pull in a reception at the Vols' 10. Less than 1 minute remained on the scoreboard clock and the Sugar Bowl crowd was growing wild.

Finally, the Vols defensive line began to put a lot of pressure on Keithly and he hurried a pass that Jim Powell intercepted to end Tulsa's threat.

After the game, sportswriters asked Tulsa coach Henry Franka as to why Dobbs was not in there pitching late in the fourth quarter. He merely said, "He

when Denver Crawford, a husky tackle, blocked a Dobbs punt and the ball flew out of the end zone for a safety.

In the fourth quarter, Ig Fuson put the Vols safely ahead for good, 14-6, when he scored from the Tulsa 2. It was the biggest touchdown that

Tulsa quarterback Glenn Dobbs races for open field against the Vols.

Ig Fuson's fourth-quarter touchdown secured the Volunteers' win over Tulsa.

(Dobbs) wasn't hurt" and let it go at that.

The recital of the obstacles (not to mention Dobbs and his arm and toe) that Tennessee had to overcome were legion. An apparent touchdown pass from Slater to Al Hust was ruled incomplete because the play had started a split second after the first half had ended. A cinch fourth-quarter touchdown was denied the Vols due to Fuson's fumble at the Tulsa 4.

Tulsa was primarily a passing team and fell short of the Vols in manpower. The game's final stats proved it, too. The Golden Hurricanes gained 168 yards through the air, but lost 39 yards rushing. Tennessee wrapped up its performance with 296 yards from both the ground and air game.

Vols fans can now bury the ghosts of that loss to Boston College in the 1941 Sugar Bowl. While they're at it, Vols fans may also want to bury the haunting memories of Glenn Dobbs and the great Tulsa Aerial Circus that almost pinned another Sugar Bowl loss on them.

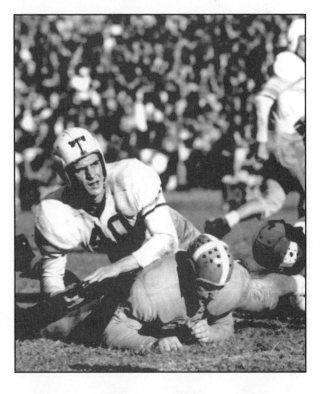

The 1946 Volunteers posted a 9-2 record and won the SEC title.

Vols Hold Back Tide & Gilmer

Alabama	0	0	0	0	–	0
Tennessee	6	0	6	0	–	12

By Walter Stewart
The Commercial Appeal

KNOXVILLE, Oct. 19, 1946

A labama's legendary Crimson Tide surged four times against a stiff orange wall this afternoon and was rolled back all four times. When dusk arrived, it smudged clean a scoreboard with Tennessee 12, Alabama 0, drawn across it.

Riding in behind the ballistically perfect arm of Harry Gilmer, the Crimson Tide traveled to inside the

Bob Lund had a punting duel with Alabama's **Harry Gilmer.**

Tennessee 10-yard line four times in a game which cobbled the spines of 40,000 with steady delirium as Tennessee rose to one bruising climax after another.

The Tennessee line was the difference this time — a muscle-laced orange army which throttled the Alabama running attack and gunned through to hurry Gilmer just enough to dull the edge of a passing show that produced 16 completions and 157 yards for the Tide.

Bob Lund was the leather tip of the Tennessee javelin which twice pierced a craggy Alabama defense on marches of 68 and 46 yards.

In the final period, Gilmer lifted the Tide to an attacking tempo almost unequalled in the history of Southern football and carried them on passing forays of 57, 47 and 29 yards, only to see the Red Elephants perish in a crowd of orange arms. The Vols were not too stubborn defensively outside the 10-yard line, but once the Tide reached that point the Vols were bedded in concrete.

It was the 38th successive regular-season victory for Neyland's Vols and Alabama's first defeat since Georgia whipped the Tide, 14-7, in November 1944.

Although Alabama failed to put up enough winning numbers on the scoreboard, it did rack up some fancy stats. The Tide put together 14 first downs to the Vols' 9. On the ground, Tennessee rushed for 120 yards to Alabama's 69. However, in the air, the Vols completed 4 of nine passes for 55 yards. Gilmer & Co. overshadowed them with 16 completions in 36 attempts for 157 yards.

Dick Huffman was a consensus All-American tackle in 1946.

Bob Lund scored both of Tennessee's touchdowns against the Crimson Tide.

Late in the first quarter, Gilmer intercepted Walter Slater's pass at the Vols' 40. After two incomplete passes, he pegged Lowell Tew at the Vols' 10. With clouds gathering, Gilmer raced off tackle only to be met by George Balitsaris at the Vols' 7. Balitsaris' jarring tackle both knocked the ball loose and allowed him to make the fumble recovery. It also turned the Tide back.

In the second quarter, the Vols began a march at the Alabama 44 with a flurry of contusions and abrasions. Lund started the drive by cutting back over left guard for eight yards. Bill Gold and Lund then alternated carrying the ball to the Tide 21. Lund next passed to Billy Hillman at the Tide 8.

With a first down, the Vols mixed it up and sent Hillman on a reverse inside left tackle down to the Tide 3. Lund powered over for the remaining yardage for a touchdown to put Tennessee ahead, 6-0. Charley Mitchell missed the point-after attempt.

Midway through the third period, Tennessee got hot. Beginning at their 43, the Vols got a break when the Tide was penalized 15 yards. Slater then pitched a 32-yard pass to Jim Powell at the Tide 13. Gold rammed up the middle for two yards and Slater found a gap over right tackle for 8 yards. Lund then smashed in for the touchdown to give Tennessee a 12-0 lead. Alabama's Jim Cain blocked Hillman's point-after kick.

Gilmer took over at that point and began the Tide's many assaults on the Vols' end zone.

Like a champion, Tennessee beat back the Tide's raiding punches.

Vols Trip Kentucky in Icy Thriller

| Kentucky | 0 | 0 | 0 | 0 | – | 0 |
| Tennessee | 0 | 7 | 0 | 0 | – | 7 |

By Walter Stewart
The Commercial Appeal

KNOXVILLE, Nov. 25, 1950

Kentucky's Wildcats, who have averaged a point a season against Gen. Robert Neyland's teams through 18 bitter years, fell off that searing pace on this arctic afternoon as Tennessee's Vols held on to win, 7-0.

Sculptured in temperature 10 degrees above zero, this magnificently-earned triumph ripped the Wildcats' undefeated campaign into shabby rags and warmed the hearts, if not the bodies, of 45,000 pneumonia seekers. The last ticket was sold more than two weeks ago and the 5,000 who remained sedately at home avoided one of the most primitive encounters in Tennessee Vols football history.

Tennessee drew Wildcat blood in the second quarter when hustlin' Hank Lauricella gunned a 27-yard fourth-down pass into Bert Rechichar's refrigerated hands as he cut across the flagged corner of the end zone. Pat Shires' conversion pass gave the Vols a 7-0 lead — and all of the points they would need.

On the second play of the fourth quarter, Tennessee's assault was stopped at the Kentucky 1-foot stripe. The anguished Cats, however, were never able to get past the Vols' 30. Still, Bear Bryant's boys managed to mix the bitter with the sweet by accepting a Sugar Bowl bid after their defeat.

The Vols rushed for 131 yards while the Cats' ground

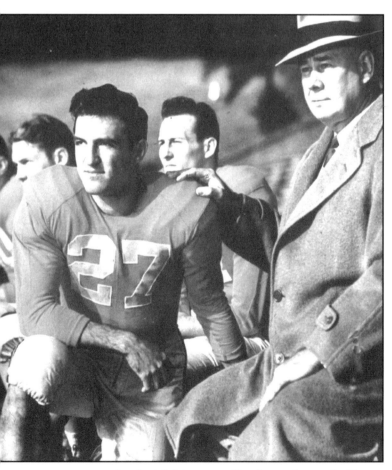

Neyland with his star tailback, Hank Lauricella, who threw the winning pass to Bert Rechichar.

Pat Shire's extra-point pass, which gave the Vols a 7-0 lead, closed out the afternoon's scoring.

attack managed to get just 36. Kentucky, behind the skilled passing of Babe Parilli, owned the air game with 14 completions in 31 attempts for 150 yards. The Vols completed only 4 passes in 10 attempts for 71 yards.

Tennessee's only scoring drive came as the result of an opportunity which was golden right to its throbbing heart. The Vols had lost 26 yards in two plays when Lauricella boomed a punt into Kentucky territory. Ben Zaranka, the big Wildcat end, exploded into a block and was wallowing on the turf when the ball bounced into his leg and quickly recovered by Vols center Bob Davis.

On the first play following the recovery, Herky Payne skirted right end for 12 yards. He went for six more yards over right tackle, then Andy Kozar lost five yards on a fumble which the Vols recovered. After a 5-yard delay of game penalty was leveled against the Vols, Lauricella drifted to his left while wingback Rechichar knifed down the field to the right. He was well covered by a pair of Cat defenders. But Lauricella fired a pinpoint pass to Rechichar deep in the end zone for the touchdown. Shires, who had kicked 30 of 33 previous

attempts, missed the goal posts. However, a Kentucky penalty gave him a second chance and Shires made it to give the Vols a 7-0 lead.

In the fourth quarter, Parilli & Co. made a final attempt to reach the Vols' end zone. Beginning at the Cats' 21, Parilli connected with Al Bruno on a 15-yard pass. Parilli then rambled for 13 yards around right end. Dom Fucci added 15 yards to move the ball to the Vols' 36. After a 5-yard penalty against the Cats, Parilli passed to Bruno for a 10-yard gain to move the ball to the Vols' 31.

Parilli missed on two passing attempts and a poor center snap caused a fumble which Kentucky All-American tackle Bob Gain fell on at the Vols' 37.

On the first pass, the Tennessee defense rose to a feverish crest. Blasting through, Jack Stroud pinned Parilli for a 9-yard loss. Then Ted Daffer sacked him while attempting to pass for a 5-yard loss.

On fourth down, Parilli was badly rushed and threw so wildly that the Vols' Gordon Polofsky intercepted his pass and returned it to the Kentucky 43.

Afterwards, the Vols and Lauricella ran out the clock.

Vols Rally to Defeat Longhorns, 20-14

By Walter Stewart
The Commercial Appeal

DALLAS, Jan. 1, 1951

The University of Texas Longhorns' football team is in the market for a new pair of front teeth because theirs were kicked out by Tennessee this dank afternoon as the Orangemen slashed a 20-14 victory over the Texans in front of a rain-soaked crowd of 75,000 at the Cotton Bowl.

Outweighed 27 pounds to a man in the offensive and defensive lines, the Vols battled a Texas squad which local sportswriters believed capable of running the ragged mountain boys home with shirt tails in flames.

Behind, 14-7, in the first half, the Vols came back with thunder and completely controlled the second half by using a lacerating ground attack that featured fullback Andy Kozar. The Vols then marched 83 yards over rumpled Longhorn bodies to narrow the score to 14-13 and journeyed 80 yards downfield once more to put Tennessee ahead for good, 20-14.

Andy Kozar plowed through the middle of the Texas defense for a 1-yard game-winning touchdown.

Tennessee	7	0	0	13	– 20
Texas	0	14	0	0	– 14

The Vols at practice prior to their 1951 Cotton Bowl meeting with Texas.

Tennessee struck first when Hank Lauricella looped right end and cut a 75-yard path through the Texas secondary to put the ball on the Longhorns' 5-yard line. Three plays later, Herky Payne lobbed a pass to John Gruble in the end zone for the touchdown. Pat Shires' extra-point kick gave the Vols a 7-0 lead.

At the beginning of the second quarter, Tennessee had been backed up to their 1-yard line when Texas' Jim Lansford blocked a Lauricella punt and Longhorns linebacker Don Cunningham fell on it at the Vols' 8.

Three Texas ground attempts by Byron Townsend and Bubba Shands covered only 3 yards. And when Tennessee fans thought the end zone had been saved,

Townsend took a pitchout and banged over for the touchdown. Ben Tompkins booted the point-after kick to even the score at 7-7.

On their next series, the Texans went all the way.

Tompkins got the drive started by hitting Tom Stolhandske with a jump pass for 16 yards and Townsend added six more.

Tompkins then faked a button-hook pass to Stolhandske, raced back and drilled a 45-yard pass into the right end zone to Gil Dawson, who outleaped two defenders for the pass. Tompkins' point-after kick gave the Longhorns a 14-7 lead.

At halftime, with Texas in firm control, Tennessee coach Bob Neyland must have spoken sharply to his troops, because the Vols mounted a razzle-dazzle

LAURICELLA 3 YDS PAST LINE OF SCRIMMAGE ON 75 YD RUN AGAINST TEXAS IN COTTON BOWL JANUARY 1st 1951

HAHN HITS MENASCO

KOZAR TAKES OUT GEORGES

LYONS DELAYS McFADIN

MICHELS HEADS FOR DILLON

RECHICHAR AND KASETA FLATTEN DAVIS

CUNNINGHAM AVOIDS STROUD, FINALLY MAKES TACKLE 70 YARDS DOWN FIELD

GRUBLE LUNGES TOWARD OCHOA

attack which hasn't been seen in the hills of East Tennessee since the university in Knoxville had been built.

There were double handoffs with the quarterback and fullback swapping the ball, pitchouts from the buck-lateral and criss-crossing reverses. And they began to pay big dividends.

At the end of the third quarter, Texas' Billy Don Porter punted to the Vols' 17 and Tennessee got cracking. Six plays moved the ball to the Texas 47.

With the game moving into the final quarter, Lauricella slammed over left tackle for six yards and Kozar hit the same hole and added 15 yards.

Kozar pounded the left side of the Texas defense again and picked up 12 more yards to the Longhorns' 19.

Continuing to pick on the same weakness of the Texas defense, Kosar burst through to the Longhorns' 5 and spun off right guard to find the end zone waiting with open arms. Shires missed his fifth extra point of the season and Tennessee trailed, 14-13.

When Texas got the ball, Tomkins led an attack which reached the Vols' 36. But a Tompkins' pass was intercepted at the Vols' 20 by Cowboy Hill, who ripped down the sideline to the Longhorns' 46 to put Tennessee back in striking distance. It was also the play upon which the game pivoted — for Tennessee was not to be denied or even slowed down.

But it didn't seem to be because Kosar fumbled at the Longhorns' 36. Yet one play later, Dawson was tackled by a mob of Vols and the ball squirted loose, with Hill making the recovery for Tennessee at the Longhorns' 43.

Kosar wasted no time in picking up six yards, then Lauricella passed to Rechichar on the Texas 13 and ran over left tackle to the 1-yard line. Kosar lunged over the middle of the Tennessee line for the touchdown. And this time Shires booted the extra-point kick which gave the Vols a 20-14 lead.

Texas attempted a late rally by driving from the Longhorns' 35 to the Vols' 17, but the Tennessee defense stiffened and turned back the Texans.

It was a game for the ages.

new year's day

1951

Cotton Bowl!

UNIVERSITY OF TENNESSEE vs UNIVERSITY OF TEXAS

50c

Vandy Gives No.1 Volunteers Scare in 35-27 Thriller

Vanderbilt	0	0	20	7	–	27
Tennessee	7	7	7	14	–	35

Doug Atkins

By Escar Thompson
The Commercial Appeal

KNOXVILLE, Dec. 1, 1951

A fighting Vanderbilt football team, fired to great heights by the sensational passing of quarterback Bill Wade, gave mighty Tennessee a real scare today before bowing, 35-27.

A wildly screaming crowd of 45,000 homecoming fans shouted itself hoarse as Wade riddled unbeaten Tennessee's secondary with passes and almost pulled off the biggest upset of the season.

The bitterly-fought game ended in a free-for-all which was quickly brought under control by officials, coaches and police.

The hard-won victory was the 10th straight of the season for the Sugar Bowl-bound Volunteers and

Andy Kozar

THE UNIVERSITY OF TENNESSEE NATIONAL ALUMNI ASSOCIATION

A tradition of service to alumni from Chattanooga, Knoxville, Martin, and Memphis since 1836.

January 1, 1999

Dear Tennessee Traveler:

It's a great pleasure to welcome you to the Hilton Pointe Squaw Peak!

We recognize you had a choice of options when choosing travel to the 1999 Fiesta Bowl and we are glad you decided to travel on the Official UT National Alumni Association package. Accordingly, we present the attached book **Greatest Moments in Tennessee Vols Football History** with our sincere appreciation.

This has been a year of firsts for the Tennessee Volunteers. This is the first time in school history Tennessee was 11-0 in regular season play (of course, the win over Mississippi State in the SEC Championship game makes UT a first ever 12-0). The 1938 team is the only team to finish with a perfect 11-0 mark, including a bowl win. With an 8-0 SEC mark, Tennessee also completed its first perfect league slate since 1967 when UT finished 6-0. This year's 41-0 blanking of Vanderbilt was its first shutout in 31 games. The biggest first playing in the first ever college football unified National Championship game.

This is also a year of endings--our losing streak to Florida (who will ever forget that game?). This also the last season for the Voice of the Vols John Ward to broadcast UT football games. His trademark introduction "It's football time in Tennessee" will always be remembered by Vol faithful.

We hope you will enjoy your time in the Phoenix/Scottsdale/Tempe area. Our game Monday night will be the first time we have met Florida State in football since 1958. So get out your orange, practice your best rendition of Rocky Top and get ready to cheer our Volunteers to victory.

Sincerely,

Hunter Wright
President
National Alumni
Association

Phillip Fulmer
Head Football
Coach

John Ward
Vol Network

600 Andy Holt Tower

Knoxville, TN 37996-0160

423·974-3011

FAX: 423·974-2663

The 1951 Vols posted a 10-1 record and were crowned National Champions for the second straight season.

marked their first unbeaten and untied season since 1940. It was also their 20th consecutive win over a two-year period.

Wade completed 16 of 21 passes for 251 yards and no interceptions. He failed to score through the air, but his tosses set the stage for each of the Commodores' four touchdowns.

Tennessee completely dominat-ed the first half and left the field for the intermission with a 14-0 lead. Then in the first minute of the third quar-ter, the Vols struck quickly for a third touchdown to pull ahead, 21-0.

But the character of the game changed quickly as Tennessee kicked off to Vandy. Wade, who had failed to maneuver the Commodores past midfield in the first half, started hitting his passes.

Vanderbilt marched 71 yards in 10 plays, with Wade covering 52 yards on four pass completions, including a 15-yard pass to Ben Roderick, his favorite target, at the Vandy 1.

Fullback R.C. Allen plunged the final yard for the touchdown. Richard Foster added the point-after kick to narrow Tennessee's lead to 21-7.

After the Vols fielded the kickoff, Hank Lauricella fumbled and Dick Philpot recovered on the Vols' 28. Vanderbilt quickly seized on the break and marched into the Vol end zone in four plays. Allen made up the

final four yards on an off-tackle play. Foster's point-after kick reduced the Vols' lead to 21-14.

Before the spectators could get settled in their seats, the Commodores were on the march again. This drive covered 86 yards. Wade's 64-yard strike to halfback Jimmy Ray quickened the journey, advancing the ball to the Vols' 3.

Vandy halfback Roy Duncan's dive over the middle sealed the touchdown. The score now stood Tennessee 21, Vanderbilt 20.

When Foster missed the point-after kick, the partisan crowd, sensing an upset in the making, breathed easier.

Tennessee, the No. 1-ranked team in The Associated Press national poll, marched 71 yards for its fourth and the game-winning touch-down. Payne, who had scampered for the Vols' second touchdown in the second quarter, smashed over from the Vandy 3. Vic Kolenik booted the point-after kick to put Tennessee ahead, 28-20.

Wade rose to the occasion again mid-way through the final period, hitting Roderick with three passes and Foster with one to move the ball from Vandy's 38 to the Tennessee 4. Duncan plunged over for his second touchdown. Foster's extra-point kick pulled Vandy to within a point of the Vols at 28-27.

Tennessee's final score came in the last five seconds of the game, with fullback Andy Kosar bulling over from the Vandy 2.

Robert Neyland: The Gridiron General

BY TIM COHANE

America stood deep in breadlines with apple vendors when Tennessee beat New York University, 13-0, in a 1931 postseason charity game at Yankee Stadium for New York's unemployed. The game was arranged by Mayor Jimmy Walker. It was the East's first look at what was then already a well-known Southern football power with a coach whose name was already making headlines, Major Robert Reese Neyland (pronounced knee-land).

The Volunteers from Knoxville near the Great Smoky Mountains demonstrated no charity toward the Violent Violets of Coach Chick Meehan. Left halfback Beattie Feathers ran 65 yards for one touchdown, and quarterback Deke Brackett returned a punt 75 yards for another. On defense the Vols were obdurate, especially guard Herman Hickman, who later was Army's line coach and Yale's head coach, and a raconteur,

gourmet and television personality of large parts.

After watching Hickman make piles in the NYU backfield most of the afternoon, Grantland Rice, another Tennessean (Murfreesboro) and dean of American sportswriters, hurried back to his office to rearrange his All-America selections, to make room for Hickman.

One of the spectators that day was the scholarly Carl Gray Snavely, who had just finished coaching a fullback named Clark Hinkle at Bucknell for three years, and would later win fame as head coach at Cornell and North Carolina.

"I had never heard much of Coach Bob Neyland before that day," Snavely said, "but after watching Tennessee play for about five minutes, I became a Neyland fan."

Twenty-six years later, in 1957, when Oklahoma had put together 40 of its modern record winning streak of 47 games (ended by Notre Dame, 7-0, the following fall), Coach Bud Wilkinson co-authored with the late Gomer Jones a book called *Modern Defensive Football*, in which he stated:

"We would like to acknowledge the great debt we owe those whose original ideas are the basis of our theory of defensive football. The foremost of these men, without doubt, is General Bob Neyland, the great coach of the University of Tennessee. In essence, the theory of defense which will be presented in this book is an adaptation of the patterns developed by the great defensive master, General Neyland."

Of all who coached 20 or more seasons, Neyland's record stands No. 1. In 21 seasons spread over 26 years (he took time out for soldiering twice, in 1935, and from 1941 through '45), his record was 173 victories, 31 defeats, and 12 ties for a .829 winning percentage. Under Neyland, Tennessee won eight Southern championships.

At West Point, Neyland played football and was a star on the Army baseball team. He was later offered pro baseball contracts with the Giants and Phillies.

From 1926 through the first two games of the 1933 season, his teams won 63, lost 2 and tied 5. The losses were to Vanderbilt, 20-3, in the eighth game of the 1926 season, and to Alabama, 18-16, in the fourth game of the 1930 season. The five ties were three with Kentucky and two with Vanderbilt. And the string of 70 games included two undefeated runs of 33 and 28. In one stretch, the Vols lost only once in 62 games.

For some reason, however — in at least two cases he was outpersonneled — success eluded Neyland in postseason Bowl games. His teams won only two of seven, from Oklahoma, 17-0, in the 1939 Orange Bowl and from Texas, 20-l4, in the 1951 Cotton Bowl.

It was the success of Neyland's teams that made necessary the enlargement of what was then known as Shields-Watkins Stadium, accommodating only 3,200, to the current 102,544 known as Neyland Stadium.

To Robert Reese Neyland III, a football game was a series of accidents and mistakes and the team that best avoided them and resisted their consequences would almost invariably win.

Neyland did not want his teams to have possession of the ball inside their own 30-yard line. He was the No. 1 High Apostle of vertical field position; the farther from the opponents' goal line you put the ball in play, the greater the number of plays you had to run off, and the greater the chance, by law of averages, for a misplay.

He preached and his teams proved repeatedly that there were more ways of scoring on defense than on offense.

"On offense," he pointed out, "you can score three ways: on a run, a pass or a kick. On defense, you can score four ways: by intercepting a pass, by forcing a fumble and catching the ball in midair, by blocking a kick and by returning a kick. The psychological shock of being scored on any of those ways is so profound that a team so scored on rarely is able to rally for victory."

HARVEY ROBINSON IKE PEEL CHAN CALDWELL GEN NEYLAND RALPH CHAUNCY "BURR" WEST MICKEY O'BRIEN "TRAINER"

"FARMER" JOHNSON AL HUST

Neyland's last coaching staff in 1952. The Vols posted a record of 8-2-1.

Neyland, by repeated proof and victory, was able to convince his team, as no coach before or after him, that the keys lay in — and in this order — a sound kicking game, a containing defense, and, say, a couple of dozen plays all thoroughly learned, meaning that none of them is run in a game until it has been practiced at least 500 times.

No coach before or after him had a keener understanding of the kicking game in all its ramifications. The ball shall be snapped and punted in two seconds. The punt shall be high and cover at least 35 yards from the line of scrimmage so that the receiver must call for a fair catch or the coverage will sew him up, perhaps even force a fumble. The punt in enemy territory, from his 45- to 35-yard line, shall be angled out of bounds or punted dead to the 10 or inside it.

On early downs in their own territory, his Tennessee teams made valuable use of the quick kick. "The only defense for a good quick kick," Neyland explained, "is to know how to return one." And before Southern teams followed Neyland's example and began study of game films in the thirties, many had thought that the Vols were fortune's favorites, the way they ran back punts for critical touchdowns. Film study revealed there was a definite and deadly pattern to their blocking in a shook-up field.

Other Neyland firsts in Southern football include telephones from press box roof to bench; lightweight jerseys that became known as tearaways to enable light backs to break away from a tackler; low quarter shoes for more ankle freedom; lighter hip pads constructed of sponge rubber, airplane cloth and molded fiber; a tarp to cover the football field; and keeping his squad in a tourist motel instead of a hotel. He was impelled toward this when one of his teams couldn't get an elevator to stop at their floor and as a result were almost late for the game.

On defense, the Volunteers played a containing or cup defense — they call it a perimeter today — to drive all plays to the inside and to restrict the gain on a pass play to the distance of the pass.

Offensively, Neyland used a single-wing balanced line that fused part of the Notre Dame box and some of Gil Dobie's off-tackle mechanics. On old No. 10, Tennessee's off-tackle play, the end and the tackle teamed on the tackle, the fullback and the quarterback teamed on the end, and the two guards pulled to lead the play. Tennessee's toughest-to-defend-against play, as with other formations, was the option run or pass by the tailback, depending on the commitment made by the defensive left halfback.

Although Neyland was known as a single-wing man, his early teams lined the quarterback up over the center and ran dive bucks, split bucks, and fakes that developed into passes from what is much like a winged-T. He later incorporated buck lateral plays into his system, and at one time seriously considered installing a split-T series.

"I was not wedded to the single wing as closely as some thought," he mused. "I used it because we could get quicker power at tackle."

Neyland, who was an excellent scout himself, was unconcerned if the other team knew his plays. "If they're well executed," he said, "they'll go anyhow." Hank Crisp, Alabama's star one-armed scout, used to say, "You always know what Bob Neyland is going to do. But try and stop him."

Every coach has the one game he'd like to play over; with Neyland, it was the 19-13 loss in the 1941 Sugar Bowl to Boston College, coached by Frank Leahy. Neyland always felt the Vols had wasted many opportunities to win. To make it worse, B.C. scored one of its touchdowns after blocking a punt on Bob Foxx, an ace wingback, a heresy on the Hill. The runback inside the weak-side tackle for the winning touchdown was a Tennessee play that a B.C. espionage agent had appropriated.

Nevertheless, B.C.'s personnel matched Tennessee's, and Leahy, although in his second year, just before

Neyland and his wife with famed sportswriter Grantland Rice, a fellow Tennessean.

Neyland receives the Coach of the Year Award from the Football Writers of America.

taking the Notre Dame job, was also an outstanding coach even then. Neyland felt that his team peaked too early and that both team and coaching staff may have been overconfident. If so, it was a violation of his first dictum: "The first law of competitive sports is never underestimate the opposition."

In Neyland's single wing, the key man was the tailback, who ran, passed, punted, and was expected to handle his share of the blocking ... "One interferer," Neyland preached, "is worth three ball carriers."

Gene McEver, the star of the Flaming Sophomores (Class of 1931), was Neyland's top player, although later he would call Johnny Majors, who played for Bowden Wyatt, the best all-purpose tailback. McEver, a sort of Southern George Gipp, was blessed with superb natural talent, speed and shiftiness, and later, when an injured knee slowed him down, he proved A-1 also as defender, blocker and power runner.

Today, 46 years after he coached his last game (1952) and 36 years after his death, in an era of wide-open two-flanker football and passing from every part of the field, Neyland's theories of defense against the pass and run still stand up. And most football games are still lost, not won, by mistakes, called turnovers today, and from poor field position.

These theories did not originate with Neyland. He

Neyland and former heavyweight champ Jack Dempsey during World War II.

derived them as a star end at Army in 1914 and '15 under head coach Charlie Daly and line coach Ernest (Pot) Graves. Graves' book on line play, The *Linemen's Bible*, was used by Neyland at Tennessee.

ROBERT REESE NEYLAND was born February 17, 1892, in Greenville, Texas, the son of Robert Reese Neyland II, a lawyer, and Pauline Lewis Neyland, a teacher. He attended Greenville High and immediately showed promise as an all-round athlete. He also attended Burleson College and Texas A&M for a year before a young congressman from Texas named Sam Rayburn got him appointed to West Point in 1912.

Neyland proved to be one of the outstanding all-round athletes of his time. He was an end on the undefeated 1914 Army team, and his record as a pitcher was 35-5, with a 20-game winning streak included, and four victories in four tries against Navy. In the 1915 game at Annapolis, Neyland, who played first base when he wasn't pitching and always batted third, was beaned in the third inning by the Navy pitcher and had to be carried from the field and revived behind the stands. He returned to go on pitching and win. Among the spectators was Newton D. Baker, the secretary of war, who later wrote the commandant:

"Would you kindly express to the pitcher on the Academy team my admiration of his courage and determination. I saw the game at Annapolis and am much pleased with his pluck."

"You would think, wouldn't you," said Neyland, showing the letter to Tom Siler, sports editor of The Knoxville News-Sentinel years later, "that the son of a b---- would have known my name."

The New York Giants (pro baseball) offered him $5,000 to sign, and the Philadelphia Athletics and Detroit Tigers also wanted him, but he was preoccupied with his Army career. It seems logical to feel that if Neyland had been interested, he could also have entered the professional boxing ring and challenged for the world's title.

How he became heavyweight champion of the Corps underlines his ability to turn disadvantage to his favor — a hallmark of his teams. He had to walk the barracks area for two hours on Wednesdays and three hours on Saturdays of his yearling (sophomore) year, after he and eight classmates were found guilty of hazing plebes. Neyland always maintained the punishment was unjust.

His confinement prevented him from seeing the

Neyland explains a new play to Vols' sports information director Lindsey Nelson. Nelson would later become one of sports' greatest broadcasters.

Dorais-Rockne forward passes which enabled Notre Dame to upset Army in their celebrated 1913 game on the Plain. But he was allowed to box for exercise and found he had a natural skill for it that would make him the champion of the Corps. Elmer Oliphant, the super all-round athlete at West Point and before that at Purdue, boasted of his ability to last three rounds with Neyland.

Graduated in 1916 as a young lieutenant of engineers, Neyland served in France, studied at MIT, and returned to West Point for 1921-24 as an aide to General Douglas

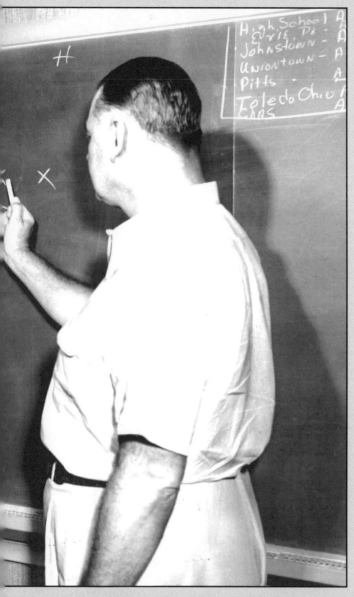

year, 1926, he was elevated to head coach by Professor Dougherty and hired two valued, long-time assistants, both former West Point players, Major Bob Britton and Colonel Paul Parker. Later, Neyland succeeded Dougherty as athletic director when Dougherty moved up to chairman of the athletic board and dean of the Engineering College.

"Local sportswriters like to say," said Dean Dougherty, "that Neyland was employed to beat Vanderbilt, whom we hadn't beaten since 1916. This was part of his job, but no such condition was ever mentioned." Neyland's second year, 1927, however, the Vols tied Vanderbilt, beat them in '28 and dominated them thereafter.

"Neyland was not harsh with his players," Dougherty said, "but he was strict. He worked hard with them, expected them to be on time, and to keep training rules. His practice periods were comparatively short [for those days, two hours and a half], but he kept them busy.

"In person he was handsome, had a military bearing, and a military method. He had praise where praise was due, and criticism where it would help."

After three years of play, one of his tackles asked him, "Colonel, I haven't been such a bad player, have I?" "No," Neyland replied, "but you have played in 30 games and you haven't blocked a punt. You should have blocked at least one in each game."

Len Coffman, a Neyland fullback of the thirties, has often been quoted, "To play for Tennessee, you've got to get 'wet' all over."

Buddy Hackman, who teamed at halfback with McEver on the Flaming Sophomores of 1928 (Mack and Hack — they were known as, and even had a sundae named after them), said later, "We won because we knew we were better prepared than the other team. Neyland gave us the edge."

Dr. Dougherty also recalled that Neyland didn't like restrictions on numbers recruited and eligibility, and in making his point would quote General MacArthur, whom he idolized, "Never make a rule that will deny you freedom of action when the time comes to act."

"We make rules," Dougherty would reply, "to get uniformity in action for all teams, rather than to restrict ourselves."

But Neyland's way was to get his way, and he usually did.

In 1938, Neyland and Herman Hickman, then assistant coach at North Carolina State, attended the Pittsburgh-Duke game in Durham. Afterward, they

MacArthur, then Superintendent. Neyland was also an assistant coach in football and baseball, and it was then that he decided to try coaching.

"There was an opening for an assistant at Iowa and at Tennessee," he recalled. "I studied the Tennessee record: It didn't look good. Colonel John J. McEwan, the Army coach, Uncle Charlie Moran, coach of Centre College and my baseball coach at Texas Aggies, recommended me and so did several others. I spent considerable time with Professor N. W. Dougherty, and we came to an understanding."

Neyland arrived at Tennessee in 1925 as a young captain in charge of the ROTC, and an assistant coach of football. His coaching salary was $700. The next were headed for a restaurant that Herman had scouted and reported on bullishly for its ham hocks and corn liquor. On foot, they were offered a ride by two men in the front seat of a sedan. When they got in, Neyland conducted the introductions in the courtly manner he could summon up on occasion.

"This is Herman Hickman," he said, "and I'm General Neyland."

"That's fine," said the driver, who'd had a few. Pointing to his friend in the front seat, he said, "This is Robert E. Lee and I'm Jesus Christ."

Mention of R.E. Lee would impel Neyland to mention that both of his grandfathers, Texans, were killed at Shiloh, and that if General Albert Sidney Johnston had not been killed early in the battle, the Confederates would have won.

Neyland's own war record suggests that if he had not concentrated on coaching, he would most certainly have been Chief of Staff timber. The job he did as chief supply officer at both Kunming and Calcutta in the China-Burma-India theater, World War II, earned him the Distinguished Service Medal, the Chinese Order of the Cloud and Banner, and the Knight Commander, Order of the British Empire. General Albert C. Wedemeyer, who succeeded General Joseph W. Stilwell in the CBI theater, had high praise for Neyland:

"He was in charge of the reception and disposition of supplies that came into the China theater. The Japanese completely surrounded China so that the only line of communication was over the so-called Hump over the Himalayan Mountains, flying supplies from air bases in India and Burma into Yunnan, the southwestern province of China.

"The capital was Kunming and we had an air base there that was as busy as LaGuardia ever could be, with planes leaving every 90 seconds. There were many demands for supplies being brought across the Hump. Bob Neyland had to exercise tact and firmness in allocating the supplies to the ground forces, to the air forces, and to clandestine forces of OSS and Admiral Miles' Navy Group China. In the short time he was there, Neyland made a wonderful record.

"In his next post in Calcutta, he had to offload ships bringing supplies to the British, to the Chinese, and to

Neyland and Army teammate, General Dwight D. Eisenhower, pause to relax and swap stories while on a ship during World War II.

Neyland with former pupil Bobby Dodd (second from right) at the annual coaches convention.

the Americans, both ground and air forces. Then he had to shove and push those supplies by rail, water, and truck to the units operating in northeast India, Burma and to air bases from which supplies would be flown to China. I was told by General Dan Sultan that he (General Neyland) performed in a superior manner and without use of gimmicks but simply through his own fine qualities of leadership and enthusiasm for the job."

Shove and push. That was Neyland. A man who got the job done.

"Neyland," New York sportswriter Bob Considine wrote, "had turned the unromantic task of unloading ships into a huge game. He made the listless, wondering Indian laborer conscious of the importance of his record of unloading a Liberty Ship in 44 hours and 5 minutes."

In earlier service Neyland had been effective. He was one of the first engineers to dredge and widen the Tennessee River and build Norris Dam, first in the chain that became the Tennessee Valley Authority.

"I served near him," writes Colonel Russell P. (Red) Reeder, a World War II hero and author, "when he commanded a battalion of combat engineers in Panama in 1935, and maybe those were his happiest days. The soldiers adored him. They were his boys and could do no wrong. Nobody picked on his boys. I would have loved to see him working on the Burma Road."

Neyland maintained that you ran an army and a football team along the same lines.

"Your men must be in good physical condition. They must have technical ability, and they must have high morale. It was tough at first to use these rules in Calcutta, but in the end they prevailed. India was a land of the underprivileged, with the heat and rains making cholera, dysentery and bubonic plague commonplace."

Neyland's success as an army leader poses the question: Why did he pick football for his principal career? The answer lies in his makeup. He was born to command, but it was not easy for him to take orders. In football, he felt he would have a clearer shot at running the whole show than he would have as a general officer.

On at least one occasion he bucked rank. In 1942, although he detested it, he was assigned while on duty as a colonel to coach an army football team made up of ex-college stars against pro teams. Within four days, Neyland's team defeated the New York Giants and the Brooklyn Dodgers, and lost a third game a few days later to the Chicago Bears by one touchdown. At halftime of the Giants game, with the All-Stars leading, 10-0, General Alexander Surles visited the dressing room and requested of Neyland that Joe Louis, the world heavyweight champ, who was a private in the army, be allowed to talk to the team.

"Nobody talks to my team except me," Neyland informed Surles, and when his superior officer tried to persist, Neyland showed him the door. The coach thought this was the reason he was passed up three times before he received his brigadier's star.

The precision with which Neyland planned his approach is emphasized by Bobby Dodd, Tennessee's all-time quarterback, later a successful head coach and athletic director at Georgia Tech.

"We were to put in a hidden-ball play for the Vanderbilt game, my senior year, 1931," Dodd recollected, "and the question was whether or not I should execute the play, since they thought I would do better hiding the ball, but worried about my lack of speed, figuring that I would be caught from behind.

"The other man in question, Gene McEver, could not handle the ball as well but had terrific speed. Neyland finally said that he wanted me to operate the play, but only inside Vandy's 19-yard line. Well, I called the play on the Vandy 19 and I was tackled on the goal line for a touchdown. So you can see how accurate his thinking was."

Besides Dodd, a partial list of ex-Neyland players who became college head coaches would include Allyn McKeen, Mississippi State; John Barnhill, Tennessee and Arkansas; Herman Hickman, Yale; Murray Warmath, Mississippi State and Minnesota; Phil Dickens, Wofford, Wyoming, and Indiana; Ralph Hatley, Memphis State; DeWitt Weaver, Texas Tech; Bowden Wyatt, Wyoming, Arkansas, and Tennessee; Bob Woodruff, Baylor and Florida; Clay Stapleton, Iowa State.

Neyland was not a believer in dressing room oratory. "Pregame harangues, as a rule," he said, "do more harm than good. Inspiration at zero hour is a poor thing to rely on. Good mental attitude the day of the game stems almost entirely from attitudes built up over a long period of time." His dressing room talks constituted a recitation of his maxims, pointing out the failure to apply some of them in previous games and how they had won other games. And always he emphasized that the cornerstone to victory comprised self-faith, resolution and confi-

> *" Your men must be in good physical condition. They must have technical ability, and they must have high morale. It was tough at first to use these rules in Calcutta, but in the end they prevailed. "*
>
> TENNESSEE COACH MAJOR ROBERT NEYLAND

dence in ultimate success.

When the situation called for it, he applied psychology with a deft hand. A prime example was the No. 1 victory of a Neyland team — underdog Tennessee's 15-13 upset of Alabama in 1928 at Tuscaloosa. At that time, the Crimson Tide, expertly coached by Wallace Wade, had been to the Rose Bowl twice, and was the paladin of the South.

On the train ride from Knoxville to Tuscaloosa, however, Neyland took each Tennessee player aside and told him he was better than the Alabama man he'd be playing against.

It was in this game that McEver caught the opening kickoff and returned it 98 yards for a touchdown that would prove decisive. "Knock a man down," Gene told his teammates, "and if you can't, step aside and let me through." The Vols deposited the Tidemen like tenpins with their cross-blocking, and at midfield McEver was clear with an escort of two blockers.

Neyland also tried psyching Coach Wade — with tongue in cheek, no doubt.

"I had never met Neyland before that day," Wade said. "Before the game in Tuscaloosa, he came to me and said it would be a rout for Alabama, and suggested that in order to hold down the score, the last two periods should be cut. I told him Alabama didn't expect to be able to run up a score, but agreed to shorten the last half, if Alabama's lead justified it."

From that day on, the day the Flaming Sophomores were born, Tennessee always brought the fourth dimension into action — the confidence bred from winning.

Had he chosen to, Neyland could have been successful in his public relations, for he was educated and articulate. But though he savored the recognition that came to him through his teams, he did not court the favor of the media, and would not attend luncheons, banquets or clinics.

When the 1939 Tennessee-Alabama game attracted national attention, Ted Husing, then the ranking radio sportscaster, came down to Knoxville to cover it, and sent an emissary to Neyland with a list of requests regarding the broadcast.

"'Tell Ted Husing," Neyland advised the emissary, "to go to hell."

Neyland's stand was predicated on the belief that if his teams won, his press would be good, and if they lost, the press couldn't help him. He also stated that he was hired only to coach football.

He was consistent in his devotion to his job; after the 1937 season, a mediocre one by his standards, he decided that he had spent too much time playing bridge, publicly confessed this to the squad, and said he was giving it up in '38. Whether cause and effect pertained, the '38 team went 10-0 and beat Oklahoma in the Orange Bowl.

Clinics and the banquet circuit missed something when Neyland decided not be a speaker. On one occasion, Professor Dougherty finally prevailed on him to talk to the engineering students.

"He took them by storm," Dougherty reported. "He told a number of stories. One concerned the time he was a young engineer on the Mississippi and his colonel gave him orders to mend the levee. He said he didn't know what a levee was, so he assembled his men and said to his sergeant, 'Sergeant, mend the levee!' And he got the work done."

Neyland's finest hour as a speaker came at the National Collegiate Athletic Association in defense of nine colleges penalized by the so-called Sanity Code for the regulation of recruiting and subsidizing in the early fifties. Thanks in large measure to his speech and the action it stimulated, Southern schools and independents formed a coalition that won legislation for the cost of living code that has since proved functional.

"How can any of us vote to expel these schools," Neyland asked the NCAA convention in New York, "when we are all just as guilty as they are?"

Neyland was adamantly opposed to giving a boy more than he needed to get by, and tossed out a player who sought under-the-table monthly payments at Tennessee after World War II.

While he was chairman of the rules committee, he succeeded in restoring one-platoon or two-way football. He was bitterly opposed to two-platoon.

When it came to getting to the heart of a football matter, Neyland was unerring. Beattie Feathers, a great running back for the Vols in the early thirties, tells about his problems with pass defense when he was a sophomore.

"I asked General Neyland," said Feathers, "what I should do when two receivers entered my territory. Which one should I cover? 'Don't be dumb enough to cover the decoy,' he said. 'Cover the one they pass to.' To save embarrassment I said okay. He got across the point that I should retire into my zone, keeping equal distance between them and playing them with field vision, keeping an eye on the passer and the receiver and playing the ball. And then go for the ball when the passer releases it."

In 1947, Tennessee's 5-5 record proved Knoxville fans were the same as elsewhere. For the first time, Neyland heard the anvil chorus. This bothered the Vols' star tackle Denver Crawford so much that he was about ready not to go into coaching. He stopped by Neyland's office to thank him for giving him the chance for an education.

"I told the General," Crawford recalled, "that I wasn't sure about coaching for myself. I told him if the public would act in such poor taste toward him after the record he'd made, I didn't think I could endure that treatment.

Neyland visits with his former star player and assistant Bowden Wyatt. Wyatt later coached at Tennessee from 1955 to 1962 with a 49-29-4 record.

"'Crawford,' Neyland smiled, 'I don't care what endeavor you go into, you can't live on your clippings. You must produce.'

"I decided," said Crawford, "to take up coaching after all."

Neyland was never much for arguing with officials. He felt that over a long period, officiating mistakes evened up. And while he was not by any means a humorist, he did have a fine sense of humor. During the 1953 season, he said to George Gardner, boss of the Southeastern Conference officials, "George, I want you to know that I'm not complaining about the officials. But Mamma (Mrs. Neyland) is sore at the boys who worked the Vanderbilt game."

"I'm burned up," Mrs. Neyland broke in, "because they called back a Tennessee touchdown. It was on a pass and we had an ineligible man downfield."

"What Mamma is sore about, George," said Neyland, "is that the officials took away the only touchdown her boy (Bob Jr.) ever scored."

The side of Robert Reese Neyland that the public saw was cool, aloof, self-centered, autocratic, proud, sometimes arrogant. But to a chosen few he revealed a side that was warm and charming. He could be a courtly man and a fascinating conversationalist on a wide variety of subjects, including literature, music, history. To hear him talking across coffee at the dinner table of his war experiences was rewarding, and made the listener deplore the General's having decided to write his memoirs when it was too late.

On the football field, on the military field, or socially, Bob Neyland lived the philosophy of carpe diem ("seize the day"). His favorite quotation was from the Sanskrit:

"Look to the day — for it is life — the very life of life. In its brief counsel lie all the verities and realities of your existence! The bliss of growth, the glory of action, the splendor of beauty. For yesterday is already a dream and tomorrow is only a vision, but today, well lived, makes every yesterday a dream of happiness and every tomorrow a vision of hope. Look well, therefore, to this day. Such is the salutation of the dawn."

Vols' Stock Rises After 6-0 Win Over No. 2 Ga. Tech

BY WALTER STEWART
The Commercial Appeal

ATLANTA, Nov. 10, 1956

Johnny (Drum) Majors, Tennessee's one-man percussion section, beat a cruel tattoo upon the anguished snout of Georgia Tech this afternoon as he flung two third-quarter passes which defeated the nation's No. 2 football club, 6-0. Prior to the game, Bowden Wyatt's Tennessee team was ranked No. 3 in the country.

Majors, who is as All-American as the late George Washington, passed to Buddy Cruze, also a knight of Tennessee's training table, with a 16-yard toss to the Tech 46. On the next play, Majors targeted Cruze again and he romped down to the Tech 1. From there, Vols fullback Tommy Bronson hurdled over tackle for the six points which proved to be the winning margin.

Johnny Majors (45) sweeps left end for big yardage against the Yellow Jackets.

Tennessee	0	0	6	0 –	6
Georgia Tech	0	0	0	0 –	0

Johnny Majors led the Vols as a star halfback. He would later coach Tennessee for 16 seasons.

Bowden Wyatt was named Coach of the Year in 1956 after his Vols won the SEC title with a 10-1 record.

The win made the undefeated Vols a top choice for a Sugar or Cotton Bowl bid.

Tech, who was a 6 ½-point favorite, threatened only once, when they were at the Vols' 21, but fullback Ken Owen lost the ball and Tennessee's Jim Smelcher recovered.

The game was filed with plenty of drama in the final quarter. Tech soaked the crowd of 40,000 with much emotion as they filled the air lanes with 16 passes while mounting two drives. But interceptions by the Vols' Bubba Howe and Bronson stopped both Tech attempts.

The Vols kicking game was never more magnificent. Tennessee punters averaged 39 yards per kick and kept Tech in the hole.

The Vols outrushed Tech, 149 yards to 134, while the Yellow Jackets led in passing, 80 yards to 71.

The first half was merely a punting duel between both teams.

Midway through the third quarter, Tennessee got smoke in its nostrils and began a march from their 35. The Vols had only thrown three passes all afternoon, so Majors' 16-yard pass to Cruze caught Tech by surprise. On Majors' next pass to Cruze at the Yellow Jackets' 25, Cruze took the toss and scooted to the Yellow Jackets' 1. Bronson's touchdown leap put the Vols ahead, 6-0. Bob Smithers' point-after kick, however, was wide.

Tennessee then began an old Neyland tradition of sitting on the lead.

Georgia Tech hadn't been shutout since 1953.

Johnny Majors was a consensus All-American and runner-up for the Heisman Trophy in 1956.

"We Wanted It And We Took It," Majors Recalls

ATLANTA

Tailback Johnny Majors, Tennessee's leading All-America candidate, said after the game that a decision to start passing in the second half was largely responsible for his team's 6-0 victory over Georgia Tech.

"Man," he said in a slow Tennessee drawl, "this one was worth coming down here for. It was rugged, just like we expected and mighty close. But we wanted it and we took it."

He explained about the Vols' passing attack to newsmen who crowded into the dressing room after the contest.

"We decided at halftime we could pass on Tech and maybe score. I mean throw deep enough to really hurt," Majors said.

"Coach (Bowden) Wyatt told us we could draw Tech's defense close with short passes and hit 'em with a long one. That's what we did."

Tennessee Topples No. 1 LSU

By David Bloom
The Commercial Appeal

KNOXVILLE, Nov. 7, 1959

Louisiana State	0	7	0	6	– 13
Tennessee	0	0	14	0	– 14

The Vols' goal-line stand against Billy Cannon and LSU stunned the No. 1-ranked Tigers.

The mighty have fallen and Tennessee was the one who slayed them.

Louisiana State, winner of 19 straight and the No. 1 team in the nation, was beaten, 14-13, by a squad of Orange Opportunists this afternoon in a football game that turned 47,000 fans into frantic fanatics.

In one minute 48 seconds of the third quarter, the fired-up Vols turned a 7-0 deficit into a 14-7 lead in typical Tennessee fashion.

First, the Vols' Jim Cartwright intercepted a Warren Rabb pass and scampered 59 yards to the LSU end zone. Cotton Letner's point-after kick evened up the game at 7-7.

Then moments later, Earl Gros dropped the ball, which Tennessee's Ken Sadler cuddled up at the LSU 29 and in four plays the Vols were ahead, 13-7. Letner's extra-point boot, made it 14-7.

In the fourth quarter, when Tennessee made its one big error, LSU turned it into a touchdown to narrow the Vols' lead to 14-13. The proud Bayou Tigers then decided to turn their backs on a tie and gambled for two points with their great back Billy Cannon.

But Cannon was six inches short on a surging, driving thrust at the left side of Tennessee's embattled left side.

This was the kind of football game you seldom see, replete with kaleidoscopic shifts of fortune, fought to

Neyle Sollee scored the Vols' second touchdown against LSU.

When Wendell Harris booted the extra point to give LSU a 7-0 lead, the Big Orange fans were groaning, but didn't lose heart. And the Vols were on the alert for the breaks they generally make.

The first one came with unexpected suddenness at 9:37 deep in the third quarter. Cannon had just pounded the ball into Tennessee territory, when Rabb went back to pass. He threw to his left side and Cartwright, leaping high into the air, snatched the ball right in front of the LSU bench and rocketed north on a straight line to the LSU end zone — 59 yards away. He needed one block, and he got it from Letner at the LSU 30, who hung one on Tommy Neck, one of the Chinese Bandits.

Then in a jiffy, it happened again. The Gros fumble came on the first play after the kickoff and Sadler was there. The Vols first two plays were losses, but Glen Glass, the big sophomore tailback, found Donnie Leake near the Tennessee bench and connected on the lone pass the Vols completed during the game. The play covered 19 yards and had the effect of a lightning bolt.

Neyle Sollee, a fullback demoted by the recent blazing play of Bunny Orr, then tore over the left side behind Vol blocking and went over the goal line and into the arms of a dozen fans. Letner's kick made it, 14-7.

Were the Tigers through? Never. They marched to the Tennessee 37 but the drive was thwarted when Bo Shaffer and Joe Lukowski leaped on Rabb. This forced the Tigers into kicking. That's when they got their break.

The punt hit the ground and then hit Bill Majors. He grabbed at it but missed and LSU's Ed McCreedy fell on the loose ball at the Vols' 3.

In two plays, Durel Matherne shoved the ball over for the touchdown which brought LSU to within a point of Tennessee.

There was little hesitation about the crapshooting play. The Tigers lined up and gave it to the player who had beaten Ole Miss the week before. Cannon, the big man, gave it his all. He whacked it over his right guard and there was Wayne Grubb standing in his way. The big guard yielded two yards but Majors, who had dropped Tennessee hearts to Tennessee boots, barrelled up and helped Grubb stop Cannon a whisper from the two-pointer to save the game for Tennessee.

It was a battle of giants that had everything.

an end that couldn't be anything but bitter to the gallant national champions of 1958. Not only did they lose to a team they outplayed, but they twice had to yield touchdowns — and this hasn't happened in nine games.

And like champions, they were willing to shoot for winner take all — so near and yet so far.

Cannon scored the first LSU touchdown, making 46 yards of the Tigers' 74 on a tremendous second-quarter drive. The last thrust covered 26 yards on a smash off through a big hole on the right side. LSU's blocking was so dominating that Cannon trotted over for the touchdown.

| Tennessee | 3 | 0 | 0 | 0 | – | 3 |
| Louisiana State | 0 | 3 | 0 | 0 | – | 3 |

Stubborn Vols Battle LSU to 3-3 Deadlock

BY DAVID BLOOM
The Commercial Appeal

BATON ROUGE, La., Oct. 24, 1964

Tenacity told the Tennessee story this evening in a 3-3 tie with Louisiana State.

Stubborn, unyielding, the valiant Vols foiled one touchdown and three field-goal attempts that would have brought victory for the vastly favored Bayou Tigers.

Time after time, Louisiana State hurled its shock troops at the weary Vols in the second half, but could never breach their defenses. A touchdown was halted less than a foot from the Tennessee end zone. Sure-footed Doug Moreau tried three times for field goals from the 27, from the 21 and, finally, from the 30. The last attempt came with eight seconds left on the clock and Tennessee was content to run one play and call it quits with the tie.

Despite his failures, it was Moreau who gained the standoff with Tennessee. His 21-yard field goal with three seconds left in the half matched a Tennessee kick of 28 yards by Fred Martin in the first quarter.

Tennessee's defense piles up LSU halfback Don Schwab at the 1-yard line.

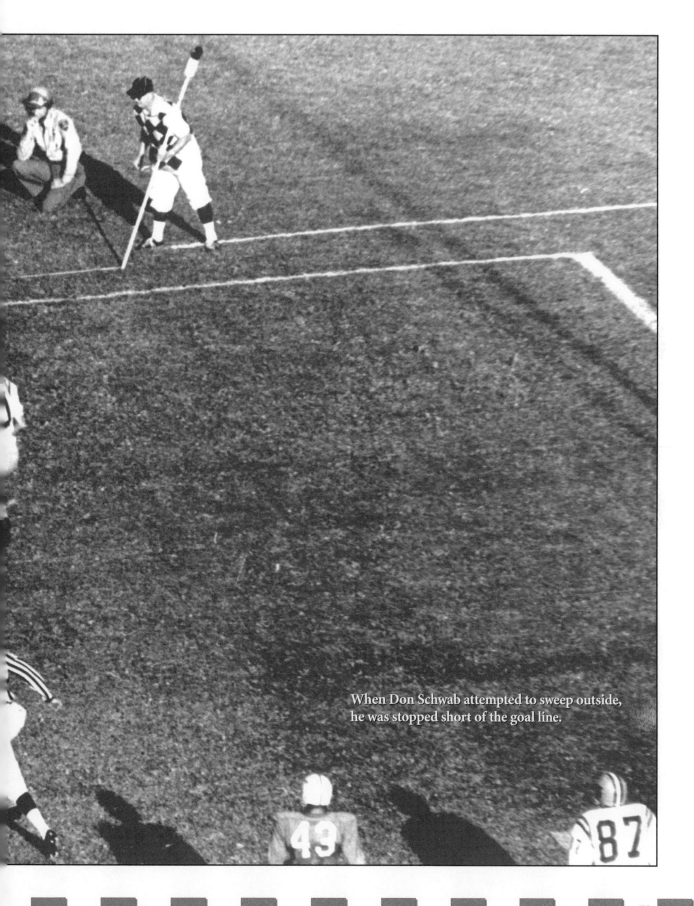

When Don Schwab attempted to sweep outside, he was stopped short of the goal line.

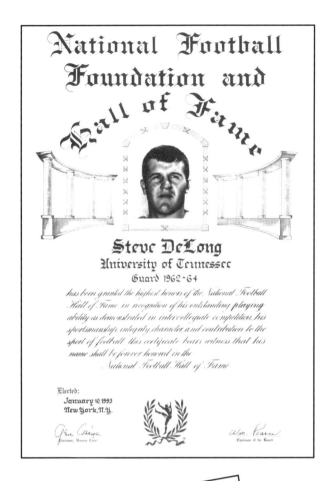

National Football Foundation and Hall of Fame

Steve DeLong
University of Tennessee
Guard 1962-64

has been granted the highest honors of the National Football Hall of Fame, in recognition of his outstanding playing ability as demonstrated in intercollegiate competition, his sportsmanship, integrity, character, and contribution to the sport of football. this certificate bears witness that his name shall be forever honored in the National Football Hall of Fame

Elected:
January 10, 1993
New York, N.Y.

Moreau's feat became all the more impressive, when Arnold Galiffa, the Vols' quarterback, and Hal Wantland, a Tennessee halfback mainstay on offense and defense, were injured early.

Tennessee never advanced closer than the LSU 42 in the second half, which gives you a pretty good idea of the game's intensity.

Ruffin Rodrigue recovered a Galiffa fumble at the Vols' 15 late in the third quarter and Danny Labruzzo earned a first down at the Vols' 4 as the fourth quarter began.

LSU quarterback Pat Screen passed to Don Schwab, whose knee hit the ground at the Vols' 1 on second down. Schwab attempted a dive over the middle of the Tennessee defense, but the Vols held valiantly. He took another shot over guard, but the Vols stood their ground, with Steve DeLong performing magnificently.

LSU later tried to get in Tennessee's territory again with Screen passing and Schwab running. They traveled down to the Vols' 13 where Tennessee held and Moreau attempted a field goal, which he missed.

When the Vols got the ball, they were unable to make much progress and punted. LSU surged back into Vols' territory once again. Moreau's field goal from the Vols' 27 was wide to the left.

Tennessee's offense got close to scoring in the first half. LSU's Gawain Dibetta fumbled on the Tigers' 14 and Tennessee recovered. On the first play, Wantland rolled out and flung a pass to Stan Mitchell in the end zone. But the touchdown was called back after Wantland and the Vols were penalized because Wantland had traveled beyond the line of scrimmage before passing.

LSU and Vols Rekindle Memories of '59

BY DAVID BLOOM
The Commercial Appeal

BATON ROUGE, La.

This isn't an old football rivalry between Louisiana State and Tennessee. They started playing the rugged game in 1925 and resumed meeting one another only occasionally. For example, they skipped playing from 1953 to 1959, then again from 1959 to 1964.

Naturally, LSU would rather not recall 1959. That was the Billy Cannon year, remember? And just the week before, on Halloween night, Cannon had run the length of the field to take Ole Miss, 7-3. And Louisiana State had journeyed to Knoxville and was supposed to beat the tar out of a Tennessee team that had troubles. But it didn't. The score was 14-13, with Paul Dietzel and the Tigers gambling for two points and a victory after scoring the second touchdown after the Vols had established a 14-7 lead.

There was a carryover of Louisiana State's frustrations from that game. Cannon himself mentioned it not too long ago. And I remember it because for once I made the correct prediction — that Tennessee would win. It was a near thing, but all mine.

There was no such prediction today and the game ended in a 3-3 tie.

The 1959 Vols' great defense slammed the door on LSU's hopes of a second national title.

Vols Battle Alabama in Ferocious 7-7 Tie

By Bob Jennings
The Commercial Appeal

BIRMINGHAM, Oct. 16, 1965

Tennessee smashed Alabama's monopoly of fourth quarter good fortune today, survived a brilliant passing show by Steve Sloan and battled the highly favored Crimson Tide to a 7-7 tie in one of the most ferocious games ever played in Southeastern Conference history.

Legion Field rocked with the emotions of nearly 70,000 while Charlie Fulton, the Vols sophomore quarterback from Whitehaven, matched the endeavors of Sloan and his stand-in, sophomore Kenny Stabler, and the defensive platoons matched lethal play.

Fulton led the Vols into a 7-0 lead via a 69-yard march in eight plays, with fullback Stan Mitchell smashing the final yard for the touchdown. David Leake booted the point-after kick.

But Alabama, down 7-0 with 3:18 to play in the second quarter, refused to yield. The Tide marched 80 yards in 10 plays and scored as time ran out when Sloan squirmed through right tackle on a play that

An Alabama back escaped this tackle, but the Tide couldn't get past the Vols on the scoreboard.

| Tennessee | 0 | 7 | 0 | 0 | - | 7 |
| Alabama | 0 | 7 | 0 | 0 | - | 7 |

began with one second on the clock. David Ray's kick tied it and completed the scoring, but not the cardiac quality of the picnic-perfect afternoon.

After intermission, Alabama drove to the Volunteers' 1-yard line only to have Sloan fumble the ball away; Ray missed a field goal from the Vols' 2 and Sloan lost a fumble after the Tide had the ball on the Vols' 2 on second down.

As if it weren't enough, Sloan mounted a final desperate march that expired on the Vols' 4 with six seconds left in the game.

When Alabama was trying to regain the lead in the second half, Tennessee's Jackie Cotton booted a pair of dazzlers.

The first was a 58-yard boomer that took a lateral course out of bounds on Alabama's 2-yard line to start the fourth quarter. It backed up the Tide and eventually led to a Tennessee field goal attempt from the 34.

Cotton's other classic sailed 58 yards from the Vols' 8, getting the Vols temporarily out of trouble with 3:33 left.

The sequence of incredible Alabama fizzles in the second half began early in the third quarter. An apparently irresistible Tide attack journeyed 62 yards to a first down at the Vols' 1. But Sloan fumbled and Tennessee's great linebacker, Frank Emanuel, recovered.

Alabama moved from its 20 to the Vols' 2 on Sloan's deadly passing. With second down and goal on the 2, Sloan fumbled and Paul Naumoff, a Vols defensive end, fell on the ball at the 6 with five minutes to go.

Cotton's 58-yard punt preceded Alabama's final threat, which again was geared to Sloan's passes. The senior Tide star had Alabama on the Vols' 8 before a fumbled pitchout cost a 9-yard loss with less than a minute left.

But Stabler came in and shook loose for 14 yards to the Vols' 4 as the seconds ticked away and the Tide had no timeouts left.

Stabler, thinking he had a first down on the Vols' 4 instead of fourth down and goal, regrouped his Tide in haste, took a center snap and threw the ball out of bounds to stop the clock with six seconds to go.

Alabama coach Paul (Bear) Bryant observes as his star receiver Ray Perkins makes a sideline catch.

Bryant Takes Blame for Tie

BY BOB JENNINGS
The Commercial Appeal

BIRMINGHAM

"The game was lost on the bench," Bear Bryant explained after the Crimson Tide's 7-7 tie with Tennessee as relative calm settled on Legion Field late this afternoon.

"The kids played hard enough to win," said the Alabama maestro. "It's my job to have things better organized on the sideline and they weren't.

"The kids were entitled to a lot better from the bench."

What Bryant referred to was the Tide's failure to try a field goal in the closing moments when it had the ball as deep as the Vols' 8.

"We had sent in Ray (placekicker David Ray) on third down so we would be ready for the field goal," said Bryant. "Stabler (quarterback Kenny Stabler) thought he made a first down but if we had kicked a field goal, it wouldn't have counted because we had 12 men on the field."

Sophomore Stabler's confusion developed after he ran 14 yards to the Vols' 4. But Alabama had no timeouts left and the final seconds were expiring. On fourth down and goal from the Vols' 4, Stabler threw a hasty pass out of bounds, under the impression that he had a first down and goal, which would stop the clock and have time for a field-goal attempt.

"I thought it was our best effort of the year," Bryant stated. "I'm not down in the dumps at all, and I believe we'll have a good team the rest of the way."

Bryant analyzed his duel quarterback weapon of Steve Sloan and Stabler:

"We had planned for Sloan to do the backup (behind the center) passing and Stabler to do the corner passing. That was the way we were trying to give Tennessee variety."

Vols Uncover Thorn in UCLA's Crown of Roses

By Bob Jennings
The Commercial Appeal

MEMPHIS, Dec. 4, 1965

Mills

Mitchell

T he sun set in the east today and 44,495 football fans leaving Memphis Memorial Stadium never batted an eye.

After what they had just seen, this was an anticlimax.

Tennessee defeated UCLA, 37-34, in a game far more unbelievable than the score indicates.

The Vols got the winning touchdown with 39 seconds to play, and this battle of fantastic rallies and counter-rallies ended in a fist-swinging and blood-letting episode near the UCLA bench after

Stan Mitchell soared over the UCLA defense for a first down.

UCLA	7	0	21	6	–	34
Tennessee	7	13	0	17	–	37

an interception by Bob Petrella killed the last hopes of the Rose Bowl-bound Bruins.

The decisive touchdown was in the fourth quarter when Dewey Warren had a hand in a game which earned the sophomore quarterback and his primary target, Johnny Mills, places which can hardly be erased from the memory of those who saw this game.

Warren pounded one yard for the Vols' last touchdown, and earlier scored on a one-yard plunge and had passed to wingback Hal Wantland for two other touchdowns on passes of five and 26 yards.

Warren completed 19 of 27 passes for 274 yards this afternoon, twice connecting on seven in a row. Mills, a relatively unsung junior split end from Elizabethton, caught 10 of Warren's passes for 140 yards, including two sensational receptions that paved the way for a field goal by David Leake that gave the Vols a 29-28 lead in the final period.

The score was tied only at 7-7 but the lead changed hands five times. The Vols blew a 20-7 in the first three minutes 55 seconds of the second half.

The Bruins twice blew leads in the final quarter — of eight and five points — but don't get the idea that nobody wanted this game.

Gary Beban, UCLA's sophomore quarterback, completed eight of 15 passes for 130 yards and three touchdowns. Mel Farr, the junior tailback, netted 97 yards on 17 carries.

The triumph must rank as one of the most prestige-laden in Vols' history. It sends the Vols into Houston's Bluebonnet Bowl game with Tulsa carrying a 7-1-2 record — the best for a Vols team since 1956.

UCLA coach Tommy Prothro, who was greeted by roses and cheers on Friday upon arrival in his old hometown, blamed the defeat on the officials.

"I'm embarrassed I'm a Southerner," he said. "I was proud before today but I'm not sure anymore."

His reference was to the four officials furnished by the Southeastern Conference, but he did not exempt the two officials provided by UCLA's conference, the Pac-8, charging "they didn't change a thing."

"We have played a lot better but not in this type situation," he said. "The pro all-stars couldn't have won out there."

Syracuse	0	0	6	6	–	12
Tennessee	3	15	0	0	–	18

Vols' Aerial Game Defeats Syracuse

BY VINCENT THILLEN
The Commercial Appeal

JACKSONVILLE, Dec. 31, 1966

Tennessee's football team picked a dark day to have one of its brightest hours.

With a murky sky overhead and a wind edged with ice cutting across the field, Tennessee defeated Syracuse, 18-12, in the 22nd annual Gator Bowl game before a record crowd of 60,312.

Neither team solved its problems. Tennessee could not stop Syracuse's running attack nor could Syracuse stop Tennessee's passing. Both offensive lines were magnificent in opening holes for two great runners — All-American Floyd Little and Larry Csonka — and in providing protection for Tennessee's equally great passer — Dewey Warren.

Tennessee showed in the first half that Syracuse could not stop its aerial attack. Syracuse put on the second-half

The Syracuse defense scrambles to get Austin Denney's fumble.

display, an equally impressive argument for the running offense. So it was that they divided honors, Warren passing for two touchdowns in the first half; Little and Csonka running for scores in the second half.

Probably the answer to such a situation is to arm oneself with a good field goal kicker, which Tennessee did, and Gary Wright's two first half kicks, 36 and 38 yards, made the difference.

Nevertheless, Warren won the game's Most Valuable Player Award for the player on the winning team with his 17 completions in 29 attempts — 20 in the first half

Richard Pickens (34), after an interception, tries to make his way downfield.

Mills (85) then fakes the Syracuse defender and sprints upfield.

— for 244 yards. Little won it for the player on the losing squad with his 216 yards in 29 carries — breaking a Gator Bowl record of 18 years.

"We didn't make a mistake in the second half," Vols coach Doug Dickey said. "We were not able to get much offense going but just enough to make it tough for Syracuse.

"Syracuse is a tremendous offensive football team and Csonka and Little are by far the best we have faced all season. I was proud of the way our boys stayed after them when they started moving the ball well."

In the first half, when Tennessee was striking like an angered rattler, Little ran 11 times for only 61 yards. Csonka had six carries and 33 yards at halftime, only to end up with 114 yards in 18 carries — giving some idea of Syracuse's surge after halftime.

"Tennessee has a real-quick team and adjusted well," said Syracuse coach Ben Schwartzwalder, "but we were able to overcome our early mistakes. We just couldn't make up the 18-point halftime deficit. Little is a real good football player when he is healthy and he was certainly healthy today."

One who was not healthy today was Charlie Fulton,

Vols coach Doug Dickey was rewarded with a victory ride after the game.

Tennessee's tailback and running threat. He ran only twice for nine yards before he was removed in the first period with injured ribs.

A roughing the kicker penalty launched Tennessee in the first quarter at the 50. Fulton ran twice for three and six yards and was hurt, but Warren opened up then and passed the Vols to the 19 before Wright kicked his first field goal. Warren unlimbered again in the second period, once hitting Austin Denney with a 37-yard toss, but again Wright was needed when the attack stalled at the 32.

It was near halftime and Tennessee started moving again. A 15-yard penalty against Syracuse got the drive going and a 32-yard run on a draw by fullback Richard Pickens moved Tennessee deep into Syracuse territory. Again Syracuse held but this time when Wright came in for a fake field attempt it was a fake.

Warren, down to hold for the placekick, took the snap, rolled right and passed to Denney, who was covered by three pass defenders, in the end zone. Only 1:39 remained in the half.

Bill Young picked off a Syracuse pass at the Tennessee 49 and ran it back to the Syracuse 29. Warren immediately threw to Johnny Mills, who made a spectacular one-handed catch while falling into the end zone, but Tennessee was penalized 15 yards for holding.

Then Warren passed to Richmond Flowers at the Syracuse 2. Another pass attempt fell incomplete but on the next down Warren found Flowers at the goal line for the touchdown. Only 23 seconds were left.

Dewey Warren (16) unloads a pass downfield to receiver Johnny Mills.

Alert Vols Break Tide Win Streak

By David Bloom
The Commercial Appeal

BIRMINGHAM, Oct. 21, 1967

Tennessee wrote THE END to Alabama's 25-game streak without a loss this afternoon.

The Vols, rising to the occasion in a dozen tense situations, staved off the passes of Tide quarterback Kenny Stabler and shattered Alabama, 24-13, to the utter delirium of a large segment of the 71,849, who packed spacious Legion Field.

Consider the last gesture as just an example. The Vols were leading by just four points — 17-13. The time remaining was 1:20. The left-handed Alabama pitching star threw long down the field from his 22. The ball went in the direction of Richard Brewer, when out of nowhere came an Orange shirt. It belonged to Albert Dorsey — and in a second, cuddled in his arms was the football. He ran 31 yards with it, scoring his first touchdown and on his 22nd birthday to make it perfect.

"What a way to celebrate," said Doug Dickey, the jubilant coach said after his Tennessee players had let him down from a bumpy ride to greet Bear Bryant.

Richmond Flowers (22) powers his way to the Alabama 11-yard line.

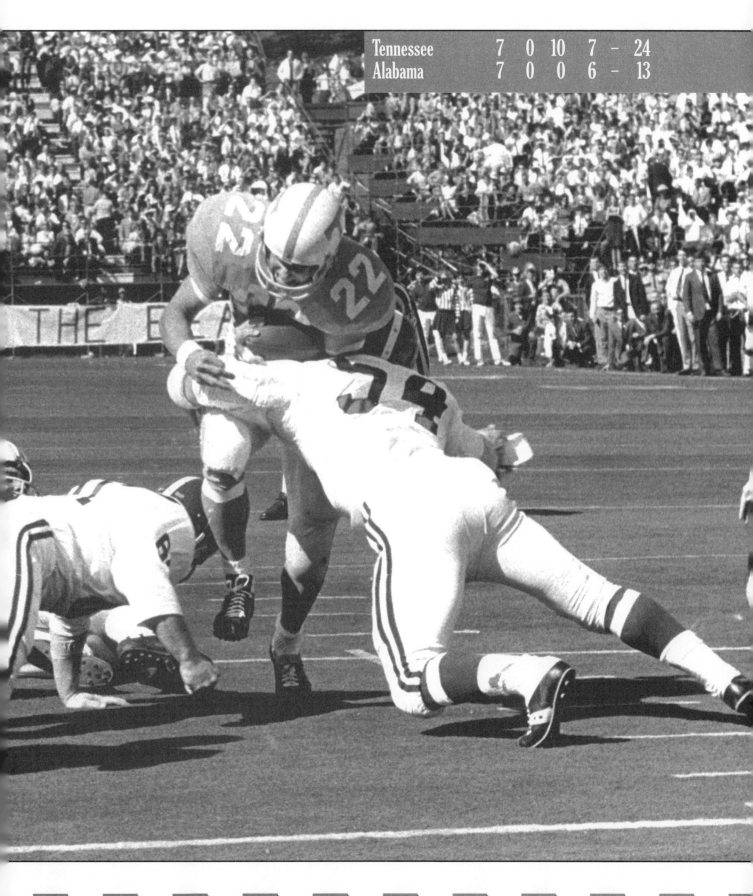

Tennessee	7	0	10	7	– 24
Alabama	7	0	0	6	– 13

Richmond Flowers starred in both track and football for the Vols.

Wyche pass from the Tennessee 6 in a somewhat reckless attempt to get out of a hole, set up the Tide at the Vols' 15. From there, Stabler passed once to Ed Morgan and Morgan punched it over from the Tide 1 for the touchdown on the next play. Bryant & Co. tried for two points so that a possible field goal could beat Tennessee. Stabler, however, wasn't able to connect on a pass.

With the score at 17-13 and Alabama driving again, Dorsey stepped in and intercepted which was set up by Jimmy Weatherford knocking the pass from Alabama receiver Dennis Homan's hands for Dorsey to catch. Minutes later, Dorsey made his second interception — and again disaster was averted. His third interception — all in the third quarter — put the game away.

Tennessee's first touchdown was a 67-yard drive in 13 plays that found Wyche throwing twice to Flowers and using his ground troops effectively. Chadwick went over from the Tide 1. Kremser booted the point-after kick.

The advantage in punts and a pass interference call aided the Tide in a 51-yard drive with Stabler going 8 yards for the touchdown that tied the game.

When the second half began, Tennessee used the Chadwick to Delong pass to establish the margin it never lost. And the long Kremser kick, plus the Dorsey interception, put it away.

Big plays by linebackers Steve Kiner and Jack Reynolds, the stout defense and the interior linemen, were factors of great importance in the Vols' win.

Stabler made a great impression on the Legion Field crowd. Homan was impressive, too. Tennessee had be a little bit greater.

Dickey said, "The defense came up with great plays in the fourth quarter and I was pleased with the way the rush got to Stabler. I put Weatherford on Homan and he fought him man-for-man all the way."

"Five interceptions — and from Stabler, too. This had to be a big win when you stop a streak like that."

Big is such a mild name for it. The Vols scored on the opening kickoff, then had to succumb to a tying touchdown from Alabama's kicking game. At the half, the score was tied, 7-7.

Then Tennessee's cinderella man, Bubba Wyche, using passes to Richmond Flowers, moved to the Alabama 11. From there, the Vols tricked Alabama with a pitchout to Walter Chadwick and a left-handed wobbly pass to Kenny DeLong.

For the Vols, there was no safety in a 14-7 lead, but a little more when Karl Kremser kicked a 47-yard soccer-type field goal to make it, 17-7.

The stands were trembling with tension when the fourth quarter opened. An Alabama interception of a

Alabama's defense stacks up Richmond Flowers near the goal line.

Tennessee's 'Orange Power':
A New Heir to the SEC Throne

THE ASSOCIATED PRESS
The Commercial Appeal

KNOXVILLE

Shouting "Orange Power" and "We're No. 1" in addition to waving hastily made banners, some 6,000 fans welcomed Tennessee's victorious Vols back to Knoxville tonight.

University of Tennessee president Dr. Andrew D. Holt greeted Vols coach Doug Dickey and the team as they stepped from their charter plane, fresh from a 24-13 victory victory over sixth-ranked Alabama.

"I'm as happy as I can be," said quarterback Bubba Wyche whose passing led the Vols attack. "This was more exciting for me than the Georgia Tech game, and I've never seen Coach Dickey so happy."

"The Bear (Coach Paul Bryant) was looking for a life raft today," said Vols first-string quarterback Dewey Warren, who saw limited action in the game.

Police, who called the crowd one of the largest to ever welcome the Vols home, said traffic moved smoothly from the airport after the crowd dispersed.

Some students arrived an hour and a half before the team was scheduled to land and busied themselves shouting "The Bear's All Wet" and waving signs which read: "Doug Dickey can walk on water."

Georgia's Jake Scott returned a punt 90 yards for a touchdown.

Hustling Vols Tie Georgia in 17-17 Thriller

Georgia	0	0	10	7 -	17
Tennessee	0	7	2	8 -	17

Vols coach Doug Dickey and linebacker Steve Kiner.

BY KYLE GRIFFIN
The Commercial Appeal

KNOXVILLE, Sept. 14, 1968

Georgia's Bulldogs jumped up and bit Tennessee right on its synthetic turf this afternoon but then discovered that the Vols were made of more than fancy nylon and green dye.

The result was a no-time left tie in a Southeastern Conference football starter — tracked out on the living room floor of Neyland Stadium before 60,003, the largest crowd ever to sit in on a sports event in Tennessee.

Vols coach Doug Dickey, looking like a washerwoman who had been washing, wasn't really concerned with the performance of the turf.

"It is the perfect way to play a football game," Dickey said in a so-so happy and a so-so sad dressing room. "This is the perfect field when you start the game and the game ends with it still perfect."

Georgia coach Vince Dooley, still a bit tender on the subject, would only say, "It's different but it was not a great factor out there today."

Underdog Georgia took it to 'em and Tennessee, getting great breaks on stiff-fingered Bulldog runners, managed to hang on until the final seconds when a kiss from your sister became a lot more important than a night out on the town with Raquel Welch.

There's not really much you can say about this kind of stalemate.

Quarterback Bubba Wyche rallied his Vols for a march through Georgia that left only chimney Stacks in its wake. He handled the ball in the final 16 plays of the game, moving 80 yards for the touchdown on the last second of the game. During that daring drive, he completed eight passes and carried the ball twice. He threw six that were dropped.

A Record Day for the Vols

It would have been a day for the record book even without Tennessee and Georgia playing to a 17-17 Southeastern Conference tie.

The contest between the Bulldogs and the Vols was:

■ The first in the South played on artificial turf.

■ The first time a Negro, end Lester McClain of Nashville, had played on the varsity football team for Tennessee.

■ The first coaching confrontation between Bulldog skipper Vince Dooley and Vols coach Doug Dickey, both 36 years old.

■ The first game between Tennessee and Georgia in 31 years. Georgia leads the series, 6-5-2.

But two weren't and those two saved Tennessee's big day before the national tv audience. One was the last-ditch pass for the touchdown to Gary Kries, a split end who had dropped three earlier passes. "I didn't even know they were going to throw the ball to me," Kries said. "I just looked up and it was there so I caught it." The other was the belly-burner to Kenny DeLong to get the two points for the tie.

The Vols scored on the fourth play of the second quarter when Wyche slipped the ball to tailback Mike Jones who flew over the left side. Karl Kremser, Tennessee's kicker, booted the extra-point. He missed field goals attempts from the 43, 42 and 48.

His counterpart, Jim McCullough, kicked a 30-yard field goal in the third quarter to get the Bulldogs back on the scoreboard.

And then the Bulldog turned greyhound when Jake Scott scooted 90 yards with a punt to put Georgia in front, 10-7.

After Georgia quarterback Donnie Hampton was sacked in the end zone for a safety by linebacker Steve Kiner to narrow the Bulldogs lead to 10-9, Georgia fullback Bruce Kemp cracked over left tackle for 80 yards and what appeared to be the icing on the cake.

But then came Wyche's 16-play, 80-yard march that sealed the contest for the Vols.

UT's Mike Jones scored the first touchdown on Neyland Stadium's Tartan Turf.

Sun Shines on Dickey's Old Tennessee Home

Florida	7	0	0	0	–	7
Tennessee	14	10	14	0	–	38

BY DAVID BLOOM
The Commercial Appeal

KNOXVILLE, Oct. 24, 1970

Tennessee squandered opportunities as though there'd be a million later on. There darned nearly was as the Vols massacred Florida, 38-7, this afternoon.

For a game which aroused emotions on both sides, there were scarcely any after the first three minutes. The Vols scored handily, and in the gloom of Neyland Stadium, lit up the scoreboard five times more.

If it was revenge on Doug Dickey for leaving Tennessee to go to Florida the majority of 64,069 wanted — they got it in gallon measures. Compassion set in early, and enthusiastic rejoicing succeeded it. The victory was that easy for Bill Battle. The brand new Vols coach advanced his record to 5-1, but advanced his team's bowl standing a hundred fold. Every bowl game where Tennessee is eligible to was represented. They were impressed, no doubt.

Dickey walked off the field with Bobby Scott, his quarterback of two years, and congratulated him heartily — well, as heartily as a heartbroken coach could. Scott set a new Tennessee passing record with 21 completions for 385 yards and two touchdowns. On the other side of the line, in orange and blue, was the sensational John Reaves, the All-American candidate. He was badgered by an aggressive Tennessee defense, threw 52 passes, completed 21 passes and had four intercepted. Two of those were turned into touchdowns.

And did Bill Battle expect anything like this? To that question there was a quizzical look and a "Would anybody?" He got perhaps the happiest ride of his life across the field to meet Dickey.

Tennessee scored in nearly every category. The crowd reaction turned from guarded optimism, when Scott threw a 42-yard pass to Joe Thompson for a touchdown with only 3:10 elapsed, to laughing cheers when the Vols' second team was fiddling around the Florida goal with only seconds remaining.

Yet in the beginning, even with the rousing start, it seemed that Tennessee, as good as it was, wasn't going to embrace its chances. The Gators didn't move the ball one bit — even with Reaves, prime receiver Carlos Alvarez and running back Tommy Durrance carrying the load. "Tennessee never let us get untracked," said Dickey, who was greeted by mingled boos and cheers.

Scott, who got his start toward the record with a modest 14-yarder to Lester McClain wound up with 21 completions in 38 attempts for 385 yards. "It had to be my best day," Scott said. He broke the record of 338 yards set by Bubba Wyche against Auburn in 1968.

"Our three defensive lapses in the first half put us out of the ball game," Dickey said. "I thought we should have gone into the dressing room, 14-7."

Tennessee, however, wasting no time in getting off to a rousing start.

Scott, harassed by two defenders, particularly Jack Youngblood, scrambled around until he got Thompson in his sights and delivered his pass at the Florida 23. Thompson, who had made a fine move getting away from Florida's defenders,

Curt Watson was a three-time All-SEC fullback at Tennessee during 1969-71.

crossed the goal line while the Tennessee fans were whooping it up.

The Vols marched to the Florida goal line again, but Harvin Clark picked off a Scott pass in the end zone.

On their next series, the Vols came knocking on the door again. Scott connected with Stan Trott on a 46-yard pass, which sent Trott scampering down the sidelines to the Florida 12. Vols kicker George Hunt, however, missed on the 34-yard field goal attempt.

Determined, the Vols mounted one more drive and reached the Florida 35. From there, Scott passed to Don McLeary. Curt Watson carried it over from the Florida 5 for the touchdown.

Nobody was breathing easy with the Vols ahead, 14-0.

The Gators quickly got one back. The Vols had them stopped on the Florida 36 when they drew a 15-yard roughing penalty. Reaves threw three passes to get to the 24. There, Dickey pulled a trick out of his hat. Alvarez took an overhand lateral behind the line of scrimmage and threw to Andy Cheney, which completely fooled the Vols and moved the Gators to the Tennessee 3. Reaves took it in for the touchdown himself.

The Vols made it 21-7 after another Hunt field goal was wide.

Scott got the Vols moving once more with passes to McClain and Trott to get the ball to the Florida 3. Scott found Scott Thompson in the end zone for the touchdown.

Jackie Walker's touchdown, his second in two weeks, was a model of second effort. He picked off a pass from the unfortunate Reaves at the 17, went charging back to the goal, was hit three times and brushed off each one, finally whirling over.

Vols cornerback Conrad Graham's interception return for a touchdown was an equally valiant effort, preceding Walker's. Reaves was flooded by Vols' pass rushers and he threw in the direction of Alvarez and Walker. Walker picked off the pass at the Gators' 37 and romped to the Florida end zone to put Tennessee up for good, 38-7.

Air Force	7	0	6	0	-	13
Tennessee	24	0	7	3	-	34

Vols Give Air Force And Bowl Jinx Sugar Coating

By David Bloom
The Commercial Appeal

NEW ORLEANS, Jan. 1, 1971

In a little more than six minutes, Tennessee had established a point. It was, indeed, a good bowl team.

The offense had scored seven points against Air Force. The defense had set up a field goal with a fumble recovery.

Tennessee went right on from there to win, 34-13, in a romping, error-filled Sugar Bowl game that belied the skilled efficiency of the first strike that took most of the fly out of the Falcons.

Only once did the Falcons rip to the goal line on their own initiative, and they were so far out of the ball game that a large segment of the 78,685 on hand left to go find more amusing pursuits like Bourbon Street.

Curt Watson (31) breaks away from a pair of Air Force tacklers.

But Tennessee was good, at times spectacularly good.

"We should have been," said Tim Priest, the co-captain and defensive back. "We were never so psyched up for a ball game — not even for Florida. We had to prove we could win in a bowl game after we'd lost three straight, and we did."

"This was the best defense we have ever played against," said Air Force coach Ben Martin, "and the offense wasn't bad either."

Tennessee showed its might as soon as it got its hands on the ball. Kevin Milam ran the kickoff back to the Vols' 40-yard line and in seven plays quarterback Bobby Scott drove his team to the Air Force end zone. Don McLeary scored the touchdown on a pitchout around left end from the Falcons' 5.

The key plays were passes from Scott to Joe Thompson, who caught two passes on that drive and and seven others in the game for his finest day in Tennessee orange.

Vols tackle John Wagster stopped Brian Bream at the Falcons' line of scrimmage — enough for Bream to drop the ball. Tom Bennett recovered for the Vols. Scott then passed to Thompson to move the Vols to the Air Force 12, but the drive stalled. George Hunt's 30-yard field goal put Tennessee up, 10-0.

The Falcons were demoralized at that point and the Vols kept holding their flying feet to the fire. Tennessee took the ball at the Air Force 42 and began their march again.

En route Scott passed for 19 yards to Lester McClain to the Falcons' 20. McLeary went the rest of the distance on a pitchout around left end to give the Vols a 17-0 lead.

All that in the first quarter. And there was more, to make it a 24-point quarter — the most in Sugar Bowl

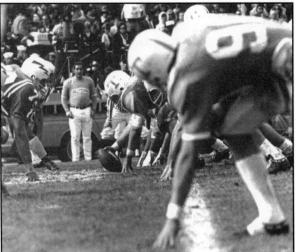

history. The Vols David Allen ran into Bream as he took a pitchout from Bob Parker. Bream again dropped the ball. This time, Jamie Rotella, a star Vols defender, was there to make the recovery.

In two passes, Scott hit Thompson and Gary Theiler to punch the ball over for a touchdown and a 24-0 lead.

Scott, awarded The Miller-Digby Trophy as the game's Most Valuable Player, said, "We tried 'em up the middle and it was solid, but when we tried to sprint out we found out we could get somewhere. And then we knew pretty soon that the passes were going to work. Their defensive backs gave us a cushion and Joe (Thompson) and the other boys were able to get in front of them."

Air Force added seven points at the end of the first quarter when the Vols were backed up to their own 8-yard line and Scott bobbled a snap from center. His fumble was recovered in the end zone by Darryl Haas, an Air Force linebacker, for the touchdown.

The Vols lost some momentum at that point. But the Falcons, despite some valiant efforts by Parker, were unable to make much progress on their own power. Their farthest penetration in the first half was the Vols' 48. The Big Orange wasn't able to move the ball much either.

The inability of both teams to keep the ball moving was partially due to the sloppy play on both

Vols defender John Wagster (67) tackles an Air Force back, forcing him to fumble. The fumble was recovered by UT's Tommy Bennett (86).

Tennessee coach Bill Battle discusses strategy with the press box.

It was a muddy afternoon in the trenches for both squads.

sides of the line. During the game, their were 14 fumbles and half of them were recovered by the opposing team.

The 24-7 score looked big enough, but Bobby Majors really put it away just two and one-half minutes into the second half.

He'd been flirting with punt-returns all season. Finally, he got one on a kick by Scott Hamm that went to the Tennessee 43. Majors broke away from the first wave of tacklers, sprinted up the sidelines, made two fine moves and went all the way for the touchdown to put the Vols ahead, 31-7.

Majors, unfortunately, was injured on the return and was carried away on a stretcher.

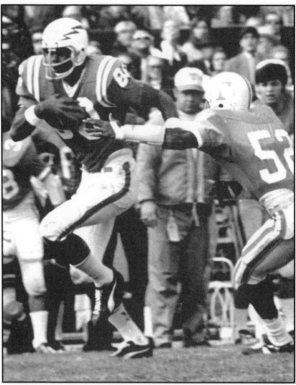

Jackie Walker (52) can't get a hand on this Air Force receiver.

Don McLeary (36) turns the corner against a Falcon defender.

Jamie Rotella (57) and a pair of Vol defenders stop a feisty Falcon halfback.

Finally in the third quarter, Air Force unleashed the attack that beat Stanford and other good teams this season. The Falcons moved from the Vols' 48 on a couple of Parker passes. He then threw a 27-yard home run pass to Paul Bassa for a touchdown. The extra-point kick failed, but the Falcons narrowed the score to 31-13.

The Vols later added a 33-yard field goal by Hunt and had two drives stall at the Air Force 26 and 7.

Vols' Defense Slices Through a Paper Lion

By Kyle Griffin
The Commercial Appeal

KNOXVILLE, Dec. 4, 1971

Gary Theiler goes high up to pull down this pass.

A re you one of those wondering where all our heroes have gone? Don't fret. Some turned up here this afternoon wearing orange jerseys and white bonnets with big T's painted on the side.

Tennessee's football team, apparently underrated, outclassed Penn State's football team, which was obviously overrated, and posted a 31-11 victory. Since the oddsmakers listed No. 5 Penn State as a two-touchdown favorite over No. 12 Tennessee, the Vols' victory must be called an upset.

But that's the only reason. On this chilly, but sunshiny afternoon in Neyland Stadium before 59,542, the two teams did not appear to be in the same league ... and they aren't.

The Vols played their best game of the season in

Penn State	0	3	0	8	– 11
Tennessee	7	14	0	10	– 31

running their record to 9-2 and stopped Penn State's 15-game winning streak.

Defense — the Vols' forte — scored most of Tennessee's points, with the offense contributing only three points to the total. That was a field goal of 21 yards by George Hunt, which capped an 80-yard drive early in the fourth quarter.

The Vols turned two pass interceptions and a fumble picked off in mid-air into three touchdowns. Otherwise, they drove within striking range five times, only to be turned away.

Bobby Majors, Tennessee's All-American defensive back and crafty returner of the long kicks, had an exceptional day and this was fitting as Tennessee honored the Majors family, which has contributed so much to Volunteer football history, before the game.

Majors returned two kickoffs for long yardage and exploded on a 44-yard punt return for a touchdown.

Tennessee took the opening kickoff and moved easily through Penn State's big defense, with Vols quarter-back Jim Maxwell putting his arm to good use. For the afternoon, Maxwell completed 8 of 19 passes — including a 43-yard bomb which gave the Vols good field position.

But despite the impressive beginning, Tennessee could not cross the Nittany Lions' goal. Penn State settled down late in the first quarter and was on the march, driving down to the Vols' 23.

Once there, Lions quarterback John Hufnagel fumbled the ball on an option play to his right and Vols defender Conrad Graham picked it up and ran 76 yards for Tennessee's first touchdown. George Hunt's extra-point kick gave the Vols a 7-0 lead.

Penn State came right back, driving 71 yards in 15 plays. But Tennessee dug in and stopped the attack on its 10. The Lions still managed to put a field goal on the

Bobby Majors (44) returned two kickoffs for long yardage and a 49-yard punt return for a touchdown.

scoreboard with Alberto Vitiello booting the three-pointer.

Now came a dramatic eight minutes that revealed a breakdown of Penn State's poise and the taking of opportunities by Tennessee.

Majors had punted the ball into the end zone. On the first play, Hufnagel put the ball in the air, but David Allen intercepted and returned it to the Lions' 15. Five plays later, Bill Rudder, a sophomore playing in place of the injured Curt Watson, crashed in for a touchdown. Hunt's point-after kick increased the Vols' lead to 14-3.

On the following kick, Lions receiver Chuck Herd amazingly signaled a fair catch at the Penn State 5. This was the second time this season this has happened. The first occasion was earlier in the season by California-Santa Barbara in the opening game.

Now, backed in a hole, Hufnagel, on third down, barely eluded the rush of Ken Lambert, his body hitting in the end zone but the ball in his outstretched hands landed on the Vols' 1, and he avoided a safety.

Penn State's punt was fielded by Majors on the 44 and he wiggled to his left and down the sideline for a touchdown. Hunt's extra-point kick gave the Vols a 21-3 lead.

The Lions then marched to the Vols' 26. With the final seconds ticking away in the first half, the Lions attempted a fake field goal, but Steve Stilley's pass was intercepted.

In the third quarter, the Vols drove to the Lions' 7 but couldn't cash it in after an 80-yard journey. Hunt added the field goal to push the Vols up, 24-3.

With time running out, Hufnagel went desperately to the air, but the Vols' All-American linebacker Jackie Walker grabbed the pass and raced 43 yards to the Lions' end zone for a touchdown with 6:33 left in the final period. Hunt's conversion kick increased the Vols' lead to 31-3.

It was the fifth time in his brilliant three-year career that Walker had intercepted a pass and returned it for a touchdown. He broke his own SEC record of four interceptions returned for scores.

Penn State eventually scored when Hufnagel passed 14 yards to Lydell Mitchell. For most of the day, Tennessee had kept Mitchell, the nation's leading scorer, bottled up.

Desperate Vols Grab 14-13 Win Over Hogs

By Kyle Griffin
The Commercial Appeal

MEMPHIS, Dec. 20, 1971

Arkansas	0	7	0	6	– 13
Tennessee	7	0	0	7	– 14

A t times tonight, Tennessee played football like it was all thumbs. Fortunately for the Volunteers, there was an Arkansas Razorback squeezed under each.

When the entertainment ended in Memorial Stadium, Tennessee had won the 13th Liberty Bowl, 14-13, before a crowd of 51,410, the largest in stadium history and the first Liberty Bowl played under lights. The previous largest crowd of 51,335 was on hand for the stadium opener between Ole Miss and Memphis State in 1965.

It was a desperate victory for Tennessee, one fashioned when blue despair had soaked the hopes of the orange — except for the players.

Two late field goals had given Arkansas a 13-7 advantage, and Bill McClard apparently put it away with a low, swinging shot from 48 yards away to give the Hogs a comfortable 16-7 lead.

However, Arkansas was caught holding and the

Hogs quarterback Joe Ferguson passed for 209 yards against the Vols.

Joe Ferguson (11) can't get away from Bobby Majors' blitz.

15-yard penalty snuffed out the field goal. The score remained at 13-7.

Tennessee, as it had all night, just could not get the long drive in motion and Arkansas took possession following a punt on its 30.

On second down, Hogs quarterback Joe Ferguson passed to tailback Jon Richardson, who fumbled when he was hit near the sideline in front of the Tennessee bench. Carl Witherspoon recovered for the Vols at the Hogs' 37.

With time running out on the scoreboard clock, Tennessee made its mighty bid.

Quarterback Jim Maxwell tried a running play that didn't work and then found tight end Gary

Joe Ferguson (11) passes downfield against the heavy Tennessee rush.

Theiler clear on the left flats for a 19-yard gain.

Going the other way, Maxwell pitched out wide to fullback Curt Watson. The moves he made on a couple of Porker defenders en route to the Hogs' goal line would knock 'em dead in Las Vegas. George Hunt's extra-point kick put Tennessee ahead, 14-13, with only 1:56 remaining.

Tennessee never appeared sure of its offensive abilities and, surprisingly enough, Arkansas never seemed to question its defensive toughness.

Errors, mostly mental, kept the game off balance for most of the evening. Louis Campbell intercepted three passes for Arkansas, a Liberty Bowl record. To add to Tennessee's misery, the Vols lost a fumble and were penalized 73 yards.

Arkansas saw its offense stopped by mistakes, too. The Porkers had three interceptions, a pair of fumbles and 85 yards in penalties — 30 of these in the last few minutes of the game which assisted the Vols in their scoring drive.

The difference in the game — and there was very little — might have been Tennessee's passing game, which racked up 142 yards. Ferguson was not rushed hard by the Vols, but their pass defense was an awesome sight to see.

It was the first Liberty Bowl appearance for both teams. Tennessee finished its season with a 10-2 mark and posted a big victory for the Southeastern Conference.

Arkansas, the runner-up in the Southwest Conference, wrapped up their season with a record of 8-3-1.

Watson To the Rescue

Curt Watson's 17-yard touchdown run, with 57 seconds left to play, buried the Hogs.

BY DAVID BLOOM
The Commercial Appeal

MEMPHIS

His ribs hurt. He hadn't practiced much. Even his best friend didn't think he'd play.

But Curt Watson was playing his last game for Tennessee and his response was so tremendous in the Vols' 14-13 victory over Arkansas that it left a Liberty Bowl record crowd of 51,410 limp.

It seemed a hopeless cause for the Orange when Carl Witherspoon fell on a Joe Ferguson fumble at the Arkansas 37. The Porkers had established a mortgage on the football and most of the second half and used field goals by the adept Bill McClard to generate an advantage.

And then there was a Jim Maxwell pass to Gary Theiler, an exalted place on the 17-yard line and Watson got the ball. He moved up the middle, swerved right, put a move on a defensive halfback, then another, and romped across the goal line.

The irony of it was that the voting for the game's Most Valuable Player had taken place five minutes before Watson made his super duper of a dash and

Ferguson, the victim of the fumble, won the Most Valuable Player award. Indeed, the young quarterback was great, doing an outstanding job as a field general and a passer, but the game belonged to Watson, to Hunt and to a tremendous Tennessee comeback.

It also belongs to history, too, and the Liberty Bowl, in its 13th outing — a lucky 13th with the weather perfect and the football game even better than that, the record crowd and the stunning finish.

They carried Bill Battle, the young coach, off the field and maybe it should have been the other way. Battle owed a lot to his players — to Maxwell, to Watson, to Bill Rudder, who set up a touchdown with a pass and then had to leave the game with injuries, to Ray Nettles, who was a superb linebacker.

But for a long while, it was Arkansas stealing Tennessee's thunder. Arkansas' defense thwarted the Vols' running game, Hog defender Louis Campbell, who intercepted three of Maxwell's passes, the valiant Ferguson, who defied Tennessee's defense and used screen passes and long ones to pile up 209 yards in the air, and his small pass-catching partner Jim Hodge.

| Notre Dame | 6 | 6 | 0 | 6 | – | 18 |
| Tennessee | 7 | 23 | 10 | 0 | – | 40 |

See-saw Volunteers Rip Irish

By Al Dunning
The Commercial Appeal

KNOXVILLE, Nov. 10, 1979

No wonder they call Neyland Stadium the world's biggest outdoor asylum. Crazy things keep happening there. Just ask Notre Dame ... or Tennessee football coach John Majors.

Unfathomable Tennessee, possibly the see-saw champion of college football, utterly destroyed 24th-ranked Notre Dame, 40-28, before a howling, standing-room-only throng of 86,489 Big Orange fans. It was the biggest football crowd (by 553) in the history of Tennessee ... and the form reversal they witnessed may have been an all-time record, too.

Just a week earlier, on the same field, Tennessee had fallen to underdog Rutgers, 23-7. Majors said no team of his had ever absorbed a more thorough whipping.

But against Notre Dame, the Volunteers looked like the best-tuned machine this side of the Rolls Royce factory, amassing 442 yards in total offense, piling up a 28-point halftime lead and winning almost as they pleased. Junior halfback Hubert Simpson, a 204-pound buzzsaw from Athens, Tenn., triggered the explosion by rushing for 4 touchdowns and 227 yards in 27 attempts.

Majors just hopes the real Tennessee stood up today.

Hubert Simpson (32) rushed for 227 yards and four touchdowns against Notre Dame.

"We have been a hot and cold team," understated the man behind the biggest grin in the Smokey Mountains. "We have had four good games and had some below-average performances. You have ups and downs and peaks and valleys when you're rebuilding. It's hard to get ready every Saturday."

Well, you could if you were Dan Devine, the Notre Dame coach who watched a team zap his Irish with 40 points for only the second time in five years (Southern Cal scored 42 points on Notre Dame earlier this fall).

"We don't have any excuses whatsoever," sagged Devine. "We played a team that played better than we did today. It's tough for us to face up to that."

Rolling downfield in an Irish-like fashion, Notre Dame smashed 80 yards in 20 plays after taking the opening kick-off. All-American halfback Vagas Ferguson smashed the last yard for the touchdown with the game only 4 ½ minutes old. Placekicker Chuck Male blew the extra-point attempt, wide right, and Notre Dame's lead stood at 6-0 before Tennessee ever touched the football.

But when Tennessee immediately thundered 62 yards in 24 plays on its first possession to take a 7-6 lead, the Irish were in big trouble.

With the Notre Dame defense disintegrating under the Vols' up-the-middle smashes, Tennessee scored on each of their first four possessions, riding a red-hot offense and cashing in on some rather remarkable Notre Dame boners along the way.

Tennessee's first scoring drive was a nail-chewer that included three third-down conversions ... and two fourth-down successes. Hotfooting quarterback Jimmy Streater zipped the last five yards over right tackle, kicker Alan Duncan tacked on the extra point and Tennessee had a 7-6 lead with 3:32 left in the first quarter.

Notre Dame punted near the end of the first quarter and the Volunteers quickly set sail on a 47-yard scoring drive that required only eight plays to increase the Vols' lead to 14-6. As the second quarter began, Simpson,

> *" We have had four good games and had some below-average performances. You have ups and downs and peaks and valleys when you're rebuilding. It's hard to get ready every Saturday. "*
>
> TENNESSEE
> COACH
> JOHN MAJORS

Notre Dame quarterback Rusty Lisch was sacked by the Vols defense for a safety.

Volunteers needed just 4 plays to drive to a touchdown. A 52-yard sprint by Streater — Tennessee's longest run from scrimmage this season — moved the ball to the Irish 3. Two plays later, Simpson dived over to pump the Vols' lead to 21-6.

At that point, the Irish began to come apart. On the kickoff following Simpson's second TD, Notre Dame sophomore Bernie Adell fielded the ball at the goal line near the sideline ... and immediately stepped out of bounds at the Irish 1. On the next play, Vols' defensive end Brian Ingram, a junior from Memphis, nailed Irish quarterback Rusty Lisch in the end zone for a safety to put Tennessee up, 23-6.

The safety forced Notre Dame to kick off ... and within three minutes Tennessee was celebrating yet another touchdown. This one was came on a 7-play, 66-yard drive capped by Simpson's 2-yard dive for the touchdown. With more than 7 minutes left before half-time, the Vols had a 30-6 lead and Notre Dame was wishing it had never heard of *Rocky Top*.

Although offensive pizazz blasted Tennessee into its lopsided lead, it was a rousing goal-line stand in the last minute of the first half that ultimately broke Notre Dame's back.

Late in the second quarter, Ferguson sliced two yards for a touchdown to wrap up a 20-play, 72-yard Irish march to narrow Tennessee's lead to 30-12. The two-point conversion play failed.

A double-whammy of bad luck at that point put the Vols in jeopardy. First, quarterback Streater went down with a strained right knee and had to be helped off the field. On the next play, his replacement — David Rudder — fumbled at the end of a 27-yard run and sophomore safety Steve Cichy recovered for Notre Dame at the Irish 36.

Immediately, a 46-yard pass from Lisch to Tony Hunter put the Irish in business at the Vols' 28.

Once inside the 10, Ferguson bulled to the Vols' 3 on first down. Lisch then underthrew a pass to tight end Dean Masztak, who was wide open in the end zone. Ferguson picked up a yard to the Vols' 2. On fourth down, Ferguson rammed into the Vols' line but was stopped 6 inches short of the goal line.

With 25 seconds left in the first half, Notre Dame was finished for the day.

blasting through a huge hole in the right side of the Vols line, rumbled 24 yards for the Vols' second touchdown. Duncan's point-after kick gave Tennessee a 14-6 lead.

Before the second quarter ended, the Vols had knocked the Irish groggy with a 23-point explosion. Vols strong safety Lemont Holt, a sophomore from Hampton, Va., helped keep the fireworks blazing by intercepting a Notre Dame pass. Holt returned the interception 9 yards to the Tennessee 46, and the

Vols Knock Off No. 2 Alabama

BY MIKE FLEMING
The Commercial Appeal

KNOXVILLE, Oct. 16, 1982

Pinch yourself. Quick. You may not believe this: Tennessee 35, Alabama 28.

See, told you so. Pinch yourself again. It comes up the same way, Tennessee 35, Alabama 28.

It will be left to someone this week to etch that score in stone and for historians of the game of college football to put away for future reference. But there are at least 95,342 — the crowd on hand in sunsplashed Neyland Stadium — who will have no trouble remembering one of the top victories in Tennessee's glorious football history.

It was the first time in 12 years that the Volunteers have been able to turn the tables on the Tide's legendary coach, Paul (Bear) Bryant, and the roaring throng — most of it Volunteer fans, of course —was certainly not going to let it slip away quickly.

They came roaring out of the stands as soon as the clock struck 12 for the Tide, covering the playing surface. They climbed the goal posts and tore them down, but this is one bill that Vols athletic director Bob Woodruff won't mind paying.

They stood and cheered so long and so loudly that Tennessee's football team, already in the dressing room and in various stages of undress, were summoned outside

Alabama halfback Joe Carter can't get past this trio of Vol defenders.

| Alabama | 7 | 14 | 0 | 7 | – | 28 |
| Tennessee | 3 | 10 | 14 | 8 | – | 35 |

for an encore. The players gladly put back on their uniforms and returned to the field.

"We'll stay out there all night if they want us," said Vols tight end Kenny Jones. "I may never go to sleep. I want to remember this one forever."

Bill Johnson, a member of the UT athletic board, stopped near the tunnel leading to the players' locker room to glance back at the scoreboard. He wanted to see it in lights one more time.

"Tennessee has never had a football win that meant as much to our program," Johnson said. "We've gone — literally — from the outhouse to the penthouse inside of three weeks."

Johnson then admitted that he wanted to make it official. "I think I'll have to pinch myself in a minute."

He then began playing the game back, the same as thousands of other fans. It was the same for players. And the coaches, too.

Here's the way it went:

Tennessee scored first on a 22-yard field goal with 13:32 left in the first quarter. The Vols got the ball almost as quickly as they had kicked off to open the game. Tide quarterback Walter Lewis, who did his best to pull out the victory in the waning seconds of the game, coughed up the football the first time he got it. Vols defensive tackle Mike Casteel recovered it at the Tide 11 and Tennessee fans were filled with hope.

But in three plays the Vols were unable to score, so Fuad Reveiz, the Vols' outstanding kicker, got the call. And he was true and straight for the first of four field goals.

Nobody, however, kicks sand in Alabama's face. The Tide came roaring back — just like everybody knew it would. Left cornerback Jeremiah Castille intercepted an Alan Cockrell pass — one of three steals on the day — and set the Tide in motion at the Vols' 19. Joe Carter took a wishbone pitch from four yards out on second down and swept end for the touchdown. The point-after kick put the Tide ahead, 7-3.

No. 2-ranked Alabama, 5-0 going into the game and a solid 14-point favorite, got another touchdown early in the second quarter on a 35-yard pass from Lewis to Jesse Bendross in the end zone to cap an 89-yard drive. Alabama now led, 14-3.

It was time to worry on Tennessee's sideline ... and in the stands as well. The scenario had been seen so many times before: Alabama getting out quickly to a lead, putting on the pressure and then squeezing the rope around your neck.

The rugged Vol defense piled up Tide halfback Ricky Moore.

This was no ordinary setting, however, and it would prove on this memorable afternoon that things that have happened in the past between these two teams would not hold water this time.

The Vols got the football with 7:01 left in the second quarter and Cockrell, who is showing that he is granite-tough in clutch situations, decided to get the Tide's attention. He got it, all right, and so did Willie Gault, the Vols speedster who is called "Orange Lightning."

Gault did what they call a streak, where he turns on his blazing speed. Anytime Gault takes off it's in a streak. He was 52 yards away, in the end zone, when the ball came down from Cockrell, with nary a red-helmeted Tider nearby. This narrowed the score to 14-10.

The big play seemed to stun the normally placid, determined Tide. It also brought a howl of displeasure from the 69-year-old Bryant on the sidelines.

Tennessee wasn't through. Vols free safety Vince Clark intercepted Lewis a few plays later, returning the pass 24 yards to the Tide 20. The Vols were able to get only another Reveiz field goal out of the turnover to reduce the Tide's lead to 1-point at 14-13, but momentum was moving swiftly toward the Orange.

Shortly thereafter, Alabama's Castille picked off another Cockrell pass with less than two minutes left in the half. Lewis — who had been called by Bryant as the best quarterback he has coached — then connected with Tide receiver Joey Jones for a lightning-quick 38-yard touchdown. Jones' sensational catch put the Tide ahead, 21-13.

Now the legend enters. Part of Bryant's mystique is that he has some uncanny ability to turn a team of his around during a short break at the half. Nobody comes close to his ability in this department, and if you have doubts check his winning record (320-81-17).

Vols coach Johnny Majors must have checked his

memory for something also as the Vols came out roaring. Tennessee took the opening kickoff and marched to another Reveiz field goal — this one from 45 yards out, which reduced Alabama's lead to 21-16.

Yet, no one dared think, even at this point, that something earth-shaking was in the making. Hardly. And a recovered fumble on the Tide's next possession at the Tide 37 was cause for excitement but not celebration. Tennessee turned that turnover into a 39-yard touchdown pass from Cockrell to split end Mike Miller who was streaking down the sideline. A two-point play afterward gave the Vols the lead for the first time, 24-21.

The Vols added another Reveiz field goal on their next possession, moving to the Alabama 21 before bogging down under the Tide defense. Reveiz's three-pointer gave the Vols a 27-21 lead.

The Vols then went 80 yards with Chuck Coleman running the last 34 yards through a bevy of stunned Tide defenders.

Majors made the decision to go for two points and it worked to perfection. Cockrell passed the ball to Jones for the two points to bump the Vols to a 35-21 lead.

Alabama, however, didn't die easy — especially with more than 7 minutes left in the game. Lewis went to work, moving the Tide to a touchdown with Linnie Patrick getting it on a nifty 14-yard scamper.

The final 5:04 proved to be "an eternity" for Majors and Vols fans.

Alabama had a lot to do with adding to the apprehensiveness of the Vols. The Tide has so many, many times come up with its best right at the end. And the hearts of the Vols faithful began to rise with each Tide snap.

Lewis moved the Tide from his 40 into Tennessee territory, working the clock beautifully. He got to the Vols' 46 and then hit Bendross coming over the middle. This play carried to the Vols' 17 — a 29-yard gain. Then Lewis tried to hit Jones in the corner of the end zone, but Vols cornerback Lee Jenkins broke it up.

On the next play, Lewis tried for Bendross in the corner but Jenkins batted it away at the last second. Then Lewis, on third down and 17, went over the middle with a pass but again Jenkins batted the pass away — and this time it popped straight up and the Vols' Terry caught it.

It was the biggest play in a day of big plays.

After the game, Bryant told the press, "I want to congratulate Coach Majors and the Tennessee team on its victory. I thought it was well deserved. I think they beat us worse than the score indicated."

Alan Cockrell piloted the Vols' attack on this memorable afternoon against Alabama.

| Tennessee | 14 | 3 | 14 | 10 | – | 41 |
| Alabama | 14 | 10 | 10 | 0 | – | 34 |

Vols Continue Win Streak Over Alabama

BY MIKE FLEMING
The Commercial Appeal

BIRMINGHAM, Oct. 15, 1983

In a college football game that one day may rank as one of Tennessee's most memorable, the Vols' scrappy, never-give-up-because-something-good-may-happen-to-you team got in the final punch in a battle of heavyweights.

And it was a quiet — almost shy — youngster from Munford, Tenn., who delivered the knockout blow to the Crimson Tide in front of 77,237 fans who probably still can't believe it.

Johnnie Jones, the Vols' tailback, ripped off a 68-yard touchdown run with three minutes left to give Tennessee a 41-34 Southeastern Conference victory. The Vols came into the game a 13-point underdog despite a stirring 20-6 win over LSU in Knoxville a week ago.

Alan Cockrell completed 12-of-21 passes for 292 yards and three touchdowns against Alabama.

Ricky Holt (83) closes down an Alabama rushing lane.

It was, indeed, impressive but LSU, despite what Cajuns may think, is not Alabama. Vols coaches all week told the players that the game had to be won on the field, nowhere else.

The words were drilled into the players' psyche and Alabama paid dearly for it. It was offense all the way, too. Tennessee had 524 yards of total offense and Alabama 453. The Vols averaged 7.38 yards every time they snapped the football from center; Alabama's average was 5.47.

There were enough big plays to fill Legion Field to the brim. Tennessee's faithful stayed to the end to soak in the wonder of it all.

It was Tennessee's second

Clyde Duncan (24) bats down an Alabama pass.

straight victory over its most fierce rival.

"This had to be one of the most exciting games in college football — anywhere, anytime," said an excited Vols coach Johnny Majors when he could be heard in the noisy den that was Tennessee's locker room. "I don't think that I have been a part of a game as a coach that was as exciting. It was tremendous all the way around. I can't even be critical of our defense because their offense was so explosive. They looked like a tremendous team coming into the game and I certainly didn't see anything to change my mind."

Alabama coach Ray Perkins said, "They did what it took at the time to win and they deserve all the credit. For the second week in a row, the defense allowed too many big plays."

Jones could hardly hold his emotions and he rarely shows them. Of his touchdown, he said, "It was a pitch play left and nobody said it, but we were all thinking just hold onto the ball and don't fumble. I got around end and saw it was open and I said to myself 'This is it.'"

The 75 points scored surpassed the most ever scored in this colorful series. The previous high was 63 points in Alabama's 42-21 victory over the Vols in 1973.

Alabama's offense was well-known coming into this game. Tide field general Walter Lewis may be the premier quarterback in the country, and Tennessee only prayed it could contain him enough so that he wouldn't blow the fuses on the scoreboard. And Tennessee's offense? It had been on and off all year. But today it was on like a Roman candle.

Cockrell had his best day. He completed 12 of 21 passes for 292 yards and three touchdowns — two of them 80-yarders (to Lenny Taylor and Clyde Duncan). His third touchdown was a 57-yarder to Duncan. Cockrell also scored a rushing touchdown on a five-yard keeper. Tennessee's other scoring came on Fuad Reveiz' other two field goals of 28 and 37. His 37-yarder tied the game at 34-34 with 8:40 remaining in the game.

The Crimson Tide got touchdowns from Ricky Moore on a three-yard run, Joey Jones on a 31-yard pass from Lewis and Moore on a six-yard run. Freshman Van Tiffin kicked two field goals — 25 and 36 yards — and he missed two others.

Yet, with all that, it came down to Reveiz' clutch field goal that tied the game, Jones' equally clutch touchdown run and, finally, some stout defensive play by the Vols.

Tennessee's defense came into the game ranked No. 1 in the SEC, but Lewis devastated the average. He has done that to a lot of others, too. But the Vols got tough just when it counted — in the final quarter. They stopped Alabama on three of its last four series, forcing the Tide to run three plays and punt in each of those three possessions.

Alan Cockrell added a touchdown by rushing on a five-yard keeper.

Auburn	0	0	0	20	–	20
Tennessee	14	10	0	14	–	38

Tennessee Stuns No. 1 Auburn

BY AL DUNNING
The Commercial Appeal

KNOXVILLE, Sept. 28, 1985

Tennessee's Volunteers rocked college football's Richter scale by burying No. 1-ranked Auburn, 38-20.

As 18-point shellackings go, this one was a blowout from the start.

Egged on by an uproarious crowd of 94,358, the Vols opened up a 24-point lead at halftime and never allowed Auburn to get closer than 18 points.

Vols coach John Majors was only slightly less jubilant than Big Orange fans who started uprooting the south goal post 17 seconds before the end of the game.

"This was one of our biggest wins at UT," Majors said. "We are going to think about Wake Forest (the Vols' next opponent) tomorrow, but not until then. We're gonna enjoy beating Auburn tonight. This was one of the great football games I've been a part of.

"I think we played as well as we can against a good football team."

Tennessee (1-0-1) won a co-featured Heisman Trophy audition, too, with Vols quarterback Tony Robinson clearly upstaging Auburn running machine Bo Jackson.

Robinson passed for 259 yards and Jackson ran for 80. Robinson hit 17 of 30 passes and threw four

Auburn's Bo Jackson (34) was corralled all afternoon by the Vols' defense, gaining only 80 yards.

Charles Wilson scored the Volunteers' first touchdown on a 3-yard run.

touchdown darts of 37, 4, 10 and 30 yards. He was intercepted three times.

Jackson, who had gained 495 yards in Auburn's first two games, got just 80 yards in 17 carries against the Vols before leaving the game in the third quarter with an ailing knee.

"It was the middle of the third quarter on a draw play," Jackson said, rubbing his sore knee. "I went up the middle and when I was tackled, I fell a little funny. I've kind of had a nagging injury all season. It's nothing serious, it just hurts. I took myself out of the game because I didn't want to get it hurt worse."

With Jackson turned into the game's most famous spectator, Tennessee freshman Keith Davis escaped for 102 yards in 13 carries against an Auburn defense rocked back on its heels, expecting pass.

The Tigers had plenty of reason to be looking skyward, because Robinson started strafing them from Tennessee's first snap.

America's No. 1 team was a 24-0 basket case at halftime as Tennessee blasted out of the starting gate like a team campaigning for Top 10 distinction.

The Vols knocked Auburn loop-legged by rocketing 76 yards for a touchdown the first time they touched the football.

Robinson started the uproarious party in the Big Orange asylum with a 39-yard run on the Vols' third play from scrimmage. A 10-yard pass to split end Eric Swanson gave the Vols a first down at the Auburn 10 and another 7-yarder to Tim McGee moved the ball to the Auburn 3. On the next play, tailback Charles Wilson hauled a pitchout three yards around right end for a touchdown. With the game less than five minutes

old, the Vols led, 7-0.

Late in the first quarter, the first of Auburn's suicidal turnovers handed Tennessee another scoring chance — and it took Robinson about five seconds to cash it in.

Jeff Burger, Auburn's starting quarterback, aimed a pitchout at Jackson just as UT middle guard Fred Bennett bashed Burger. The pitchout bounced behind Jackson and wound up under the orange shirt of UT's Terry Brown at the Auburn 37.

On Tennessee's next snap, Robinson gave the Vols a 14-0 lead by hitting McGee with a 37-yard scoring bomb, dropping it neatly over McGee's right shoulder as he fled five yards behind the Auburn defense.

Two interceptions by Auburn safety Tom Powell in the last three minutes of the first quarter spared the Tigers from a first-round TKO, but more Big Orange bombing raids were revving up.

Tony Robinson (10) returns an interception upfield against the Tigers.

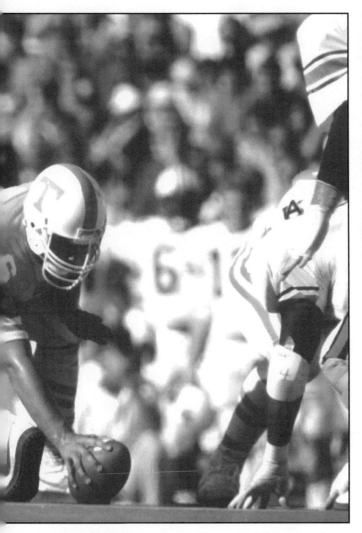

Tony Robinson connected on 17-of-30 passes for four touchdowns.

In the second quarter, Vols' tackle Bobby Scott put the Vols in business at their 40 by recovering another misfired Auburn pitchout. This time it took the Vols eight plays to go 60 yards to the Tigers' goal line. Robinson passed to Vince Carter for the final four yards for the touchdown. The Vols' lead now stood at 21-0.

Vols placekicker Fuad Reveiz stretched the Vols' lead to 24-0 by drilling a 28-yard field goal with 2:11 left before halftime.

Jackson, hobbled by his team's turnovers and Tennessee's swarming tacklers, never really got rolling in the first half. He carried the ball 14 times for 76 harmless yards.

Auburn finally had a scoring shot late in the third quarter, driving to a first down at the Tennessee 16. Three plays later, the Tigers were facing fourth and 3 at the Vols' 9. Down by 24 points, Auburn needed a field goal like Walter Mondale needed North Dakota, so the Tigers went for the yardage. UT safety Charles Davis drilled Tigers running back Brent Fullwood at the 7, a yard short of the first down.

Turn out the lights ...

Auburn finally got on the board when fullback Tommy Agee burrowed two yards for a touchdown early in the fourth quarter to narrow the Vols' lead to 24-6.

If that made any Big Orange fans nervous, Robinson immediately calmed their fidgets. He hit wideout Tim McGee for 55 yards and then floated a 10-yard TD pass to wingback Joey Clinksdale to put the Vols up, 31-6.

Auburn bounced back with Fullwood running 7 yards for a touchdown that cut Tennessee's lead to 31-12.

But Robinson fired back, hooking up with Eric Swanson for a 30-yard touchdown. Swanson outwrestled Auburn defender Arthur Johnson for the ball in the end zone. Reveiz's fifth straight PAT made it 38-12.

Auburn got the final score on a Bobby Walden pass to Kyle Collins. Curtis Stewart ran the ball over for the two-point conversion.

Tennessee's offense ate up 479 yards in total offense as they yanked Auburn from its No. 1 national perch. With Jackson first encircled by UT defenders and then sidelined by his bum knee, Auburn was able to gain only 352 yards after averaging 553 yards in its first two games.

Vols Calm No. 2 Hurricanes With Sugar

By Al Dunning
The Commercial Appeal

NEW ORLEANS, Jan. 1, 1986

Happy New Year? Would you believe a flipped-out, totally bonkers, certifiably looney new year?

You would if you were an Orange-to-the-bone University of Tennessee football fan who watched the Vols annihilate No. 2 Miami in the 52nd Sugar Bowl, 35-7.

Tennessee's Sugar Bowl championship, the Vols' first in 15 years, uncorked a Big Orange victory celebration that was Vesuvius-class, even by New Orleans standards. Certainly, the tremors were felt in Miami, where Hurricanes fans had entertained notions of a national championship after a 10-1 regular season.

So much for notions. Tennessee's dynamite defense, detonated by linebackers Darren Miller, Kelly Ziegler and Dale Jones, took the wind out of the Hurricanes in the first half. By the end of three quarters, the Hurricanes were a harmless breeze. And by the middle of the fourth quarter, they were a fazzled puff of air.

The Vols' offense surprisingly kept the Sugar Bowl scoreboard lit up with many big scoring plays.

| Miami | 7 | 0 | 0 | 0 | - | 7 |
| Tennessee | 0 | 14 | 14 | 7 | - | 35 |

Jones, a junior from Cleveland, Tenn., who plays linebacker the way kamikaze pilots used to fly airplanes, said the go-for-the-throat defense was Tennessee's game plan.

"We decided to go for the big play because we knew Miami could make 'em," Jones said. "We made more big plays than they did, and that was by far the big difference in the game."

Coach John Majors handed credit for the hatchet job on Miami directly to Tennessee's defensive coaches. Asked by a Florida writer how Tennessee loused up Miami quarterback Vinny Testaverde's early Heisman campaign, Majors replied:

"We did some of the same things we've been doing all year. You ought to talk to (defensive coordinator) Ken Donahue and our defensive staff about that. They've been putting in hours and hours. They did a great job of preparing."

Triggering the offensive fireworks in Tennessee's biggest bowl blast in a decade and a half was senior quarterback Daryl Dickey. Dickey hit 15 of 25 passes for 131 yards and one touchdown and was voted the game's Most Valuable Player.

No such laurels decorated the brow of Testaverde ... and the licking he took even might have hurt him in a big election scheduled next year.

Touted as a front-runner for next year's Heisman Trophy, Testaverde was intercepted three times, sacked seven times and spent most of a nightmare night fleeing from killer blitzes designed by Tennessee defensive strategists.

Miami took a 7-0 lead the first time the Hurricanes got the ball. But Tennessee had some harsh news for any Floridians who thought this was going to be easy.

At halftime, Tennessee was winging out front, 14-7. The Vols cavorted toward the locker room like a team on fire. Miami trudged the other direction like a team developing stomach trouble.

Miami's 7-0 lead blossomed just four minutes into the game when the Hurricanes suckerpunched Tennessee with a fake punt.

On fourth and 5 at the Vols' 43, Miami punter Jeff Feagles lined up 15 yards behind his center, who snapped the ball to upback Melvin Bratton. Twenty-five yards later, the UT defense corralled Bratton at the Vols' 18. On the next play, Testaverde buzzed a touchdown pass to flanker Mike Irvin to give the Hurricanes the early lead.

Then Hurricanes' rockets started fizzling and blowing up in their faces. Three times before halftime the fire-snorting Tennessee defense sacked Testaverde for minus yardage totaling 52 yards. And the resulting field position put Tennessee's offense in easy range to inflict serious damage.

Taking over at midfield before halftime, Tennessee flew 50 yards in just five plays to take a 14-7 lead. The score came with 3:28 left in the half when halfback Jeff Powell blasted nine yards over left tackle and fumbled at the goal line.

The ball two-hopped into the end zone, where Vols' All-American wide receiver Tim McGee pounced on it like a gold nugget for a touchdown. Fuad Reveiz' extra-point kick gave the Vols a 14-7 lead. That score later held up when Miami's Greg Cox was short on a 47-yard field goal attempt on the last play of the half.

Tennessee blew it open with two third-quarter touchdowns — both of which came on lightning-bolt shots.

Miller set up the first one by recovering a Testaverde fumble at the Miami 31 on the fifth play of the second half. It took Tennessee only six plays to reach the Hurricanes' end zone, with blockbuster fullback Sam Henderson slamming in from a foot out to give the Vols a 21-7 lead.

The Vols hit again two minutes later.

On the first play after a Miami punt, halfback Jeff Powell blew through left tackle, broke clear and outsprinted fading Hurricanes on a 60-yard scoring romp that gave the Vols a 28-7 lead.

Turn out the lights ...

Well, not yet. The Vols defense had one more haymaker left.

Safety Chris White intercepted a Testaverde pass with 7:19 left in the game and returned it 68 yards. This set up a 6-yard scoring run by Charles Wilson and that ballooned the Vols' lead to 35-7.

Tennessee's shocking victory probably set off epidemic celebrations in Oklahoma, too. By pulverizing No. 2 Miami, the No. 8 Vols probably handed Oklahoma a national championship since Oklahoma zapped No. 1 Penn State in the Orange Bowl.

Hurricanes quarterback Vinny Testaverde's Heisman campaign was given a setback by the Vol defense.

Orange Thunder Rains Down on Tigers

BY LYNN ZINSER
The Commercial Appeal

KNOXVILLE, Sept. 30, 1989

With No. 4-ranked Auburn conquered, the Neyland Stadium goal posts gone and the field littered only with a few stunned fans, Eric Still ran his fingers through his hair and sighed.

Still, the University of Tennessee's toughest offensive lineman, had just helped leave skid marks on Auburn's defense in a 21-14 victory in front of 95,341 yowling fans.

He sat quietly in the locker room, mulling the win's importance to the No. 12-ranked Vols.

"It feels good," Still said slowly. "I don't know what was wrong with Auburn."

Neither did most of Tennessee's followers, but what they did know was Still's offensive line parted the nation's No. 1-ranked defense for 349 yards rushing, including 225 by tailback Reggie Cobb.

The Vol offense pounded Auburn, the No. 1 defense in the country, by rushing for 349 yards.

Auburn	0	3	0	11	–	14
Tennessee	2	12	0	7	–	21

Tennessee's defense didn't give Auburn much running room.

"I think Auburn wasn't really tested yet," Still, a senior from Germantown, said. "We came out and established the run right away."

Still may not have thought his offense's performance was special, but Auburn did.

Cobb became the first back to gain more than 100 yards against Auburn since 1987. And he passed the mark in the second quarter with a 79-yard touchdown run that put the Vols up, 9-0.

"Tennessee came straight at us, and I don't think any team in the country could do that," Auburn linebacker Quentin Riggins said.

Cobb came at the Tigers from several directions. On the first play of a drive that began at Tennessee's 21-yard line with 12:07 left in the first half, Cobb took a handoff and tiptoed over some tacklers as he raced down the sideline. Some 79 yards later, Cobb raised his arm in the end zone after the longest run in his career.

"Earlier, we realized we could play with these guys, but that run really helped us out," Cobb said. "That gave us a big boost, a big morale boost."

The Vols (4-0, 1-0 in the SEC) rode that boost most of the rest of the game. They scored a second safety — the first came on a punt snap that sailed through the

Chuck Webb (44) scored on an eight-yard, fourth quarter run.

end zone in the first quarter — with another high-flying snap with 10:18 left in the second quarter.

Auburn (2-1, 0-1 in the SEC) could muster only one 29-yard field goal in the first half by Win Lyle, who earlier had one blocked. The Vols got a field goal of their own, a 21-yarder by Greg Burke as the half expired, and took a 14-3 lead into halftime.

"We pretty much stuck with what we had been doing for three games," Still said. "It went right down to the wire and it shouldn't have. We had a lot of opportunities we could have capitalized on."

Tennessee committed four fumbles, lost one and had one interception. But 415 yards in total offense will cure a lot of ills.

"It's really hard to tell how good their defense is. We had some penalties and some turnovers that made them look a little better than they were," Still said.

Auburn seemed to make a game of it again when quarterback Reggie Slack passed 83 yards to Alexander Wright streaking toward the end zone. Wright scored with 11:15 left in the game to pull the Tigers to within 14-11.

On the next drive, Cobb reminded the Tigers why they were losing — because of him. "I'm not as surprised as I am disappointed," defensive tackle David Rocker said. "They were bringing it straight at us."

The Vols increased their lead to 21-11 with 5:47 left in the game on Chuck Webb's 8-yard scoring run.

The Tigers would get a field goal in the closing minutes and recover an onside kick to threaten again, but the Vols defense stiffened, sacked Slack once and batted down a pass to seal the victory.

The jubilant Vols fans rushed onto the field with 7 seconds left on the clock and assaulted the goal post. At that point, Auburn coach Pat Dye began crossing the field, conceding the game.

"We got whipped. It wasn't an upset. That's the worst we have been whipped in a long time," Dye said.

Pickens' Interception Saves Day for Vols

BY LYNN ZINSER
The Commercial Appeal

DALLAS, Jan. 1, 1990

T he University of Tennessee lists Carl Pickens at wide receiver, free safety ... and now, Cotton Bowl savior.

Pickens, the Vols' resident superman, intercepted a Quinn Grovey pass in the end zone in the second quarter today, swaying a game that looked like a University of Arkansas rout into a 31-27 victory for Tennessee in front of 74,358 at the Cotton Bowl.

"He made a great play coming from nowhere. I just laid it up too high," Grovey said of Pickens. "He made a superman play. I guess I didn't give him the respect I needed to."

Instead of going up, 13-3, Arkansas watched as two plays later, Tennessee took a 10-6 advantage on an 84-yard touchdown bomb from quarterback Andy Kelly to Anthony Morgan with 6:12 left in the first half.

"That was the key play of the whole ball game. We were back on our heels and they were driving in," said Vols linebacker Shazzon Bradley of Picken's play. "Carl, he came in just in time, like he always does."

Vol linebacker Kacy Rodgers (99) stops an Arkansas scoring plunge.

Tennessee	3	14	14	0 –	31
Arkansas	6	0	7	14 –	27

Arkansas (10-2) played catch-up ball the rest of the way as Tennessee tailback Chuck Webb kept making short work of long drives. Webb rushed for 250 yards and two touchdowns, including a 78-yard beauty that gave Tennessee (11-1) a 31-13 lead with 3:55 left in the third quarter.

Webb, whose rushing performance was the second best in Cotton Bowl history, won the outstanding offensive player award and Pickens, who has made five interceptions in his five games at free safety, won the outstanding defensive player award. The only Cotton Bowl rushing performance better than Webb's belonged to Rice's Dicky Maegle with 265 yards in 1954.

"They didn't give us proper respect. We came in as underdogs," Webb said. "Arkansas couldn't beat us. I knew they couldn't beat us."

For much of the first half, however, the Razorbacks looked plenty capable of winning. Arkansas' triple-option was riddling the Vols defense for 189 yards rushing in the first half, including 107 yards by half-back James Rouse.

After Tennessee took its opening drive down for a 23-yard field goal by Greg Burke, Arkansas rumbled down the field for a 56-yard drive and took a 6-3 lead on a 1-yard touchdown run by fullback Barry Foster with 4:10 left in the first quarter. A bad snap cost the Hogs the extra point.

"We did everything we wanted to on offense," Arkansas guard Jim Mabry said. "Our backs ran as hard as I've ever seen them run."

The Razorbacks took their next drive down the field in the same fashion, hardly stopping to breathe until backup fullback Kerwin Price fumbled at the Vols' 5-yard line and Tennessee defensive end Tracey Hayworth fell on it.

Tennessee's next drive went only four yards before Kent Elmore had to punt it back to the Razorbacks, who promptly mounted another drive to the Vols' 2.

The drive would end in the Tennessee end zone, but in Pickens' hands.

"Carl saved us right there," Vols cornerback J.J. McCleaskey said. "That could have been a big turning point for them."

Morgan's ensuing catch put Arkansas in a difficult spot.

On the play, Morgan took a post route pass and outran the Hogs' secondary. It was only his 14th catch and second touchdown of the season. He finished the day

Chuck Webb rushed for 250 yards and two touchdowns against Arkansas.

with two catches for 96 yards.

"I just got behind my man and AK hooked up," Morgan said of Kelly's pass. "We knew we could take advantage of their secondary. We are very dangerous with the ball."

They proved how dangerous, taking their next drive 70 yards on eight plays for a 17-6 lead with 3:13 left in the second quarter. After a 35-yard romp from the Hogs' 40, Webb scored from 1 yard out.

Tennessee scored again on their first possession of the second half on a 1-yard pass from Kelly to fullback Greg Amsler to take a 24-6 lead before Arkansas started rallying.

The Hogs rebounded to 24-13 on a 72-yard drive ended by Rouse's 1-yard plunge with 6:58 left in the third quarter.

Then Webb produced his fireworks. The tailback, who began the season behind now-dismissed tailback Reggie Cobb and who fell only 55 yards short of a Vols single-season rushing record, put on one of his best openfield running shows.

He skirted down the left sideline and, as receiver Alvin Harper blocked his last Razorback to the sideline, cut back to the middle and jaunted into the end zone, covering 78 yards.

"The key for us was no long passing and no long running," Arkansas coach Ken Hatfield said. "We got in a footrace with them and they just outraced us."

Vols coach Johnny Majors calls for timeout in the first half of the game.

Kelly's Heroics Salvage Tie with Colorado

By Bobby Hall
The Commercial Appeal

ANAHEIM, Calif., Aug. 26, 1990

A pure fantasy finish by Tennessee salvaged a 31-31 tie with Colorado in the first Disneyland Pigskin Classic.

Only the magic of Walt Disney film makers could have dreamed up something like this.

Tennessee wished upon a star and his name was Andy Kelly. With Kelly passing for a career-high 368 yards and two touchdowns, Tennessee twice erupted from 14-point deficits in the fourth period at Anaheim Stadium.

"We could have shut it down," said Vols coach Johnny Majors, "but we had the guts and the confidence in the fourth quarter."

The comebacks by the eighth-ranked Vols of the Southeastern Conference left the fifth-ranked

Chuck Webb rushed for 131 yards on 27 carries and two touchdowns.

Colorado	0	10	7	14	– 31
Tennessee	7	3	0	21	– 31

Buffaloes of the Big Eight stunned in the regular-season opener of the decade in Division I.

"We'll look back on it with frustration," Colorado coach Bill McCartney said.

If there was any determination of who won and who lost in a tie, it should be remembered that there was a somber mood in the Colorado quarters afterward. The Vols weren't overjoyed, but there were some smiles.

"A tie hurt them worse than it did us," said Tennessee tailback Chuck Webb, who rushed 27 times for 131 yards and two touchdowns.

Majors said he had no regrets about sending Greg Burke in to kick the tying extra point with 2:25 remaining.

"I'd do it again," he said. "We didn't deserve to lose after the way we came back. And we still had time to win."

The Vols almost did win, but time ran out after a 25-yard draw play by Webb got the ball to the Colorado 16.

"The draw had been there the whole game," Webb said. "I saw an angle and I tried to get out of bounds (to leave time for a field goal try). But I looked up at the clock and it was over."

About 7,000 UT fans in a crowd of 33,458 were hoping for more.

"We wanted to get a first down, so we could stop the clock and kick a field goal," Kelly said. "But being the athlete and competitor that Chuck Webb is, he just kept running."

The final attempt for the Vols began from their 23 with 30 seconds left. They used their last timeout as Colorado prepared to punt with 39 seconds left.

Tennessee got to the 50 on one play, thanks to a 12-yard run by Webb and a 15-yard penalty against Colorado for having 12 defenders on the field. On the next play, Webb picked up nine yards, leaving 18 seconds.

Two incomplete passes by Kelly left seven seconds and Tennessee facing fourth and 1 at the Colorado 41.

The game was billed as an offensive show, but it didn't explode until Colorado had taken a 24-10 lead with 9:34 left in the game on a 55-yard punt return by Dave McCloughan.

Then Kelly went to work, hitting 17 of 26 passes for 235 yards in the final 15 minutes.

The poised junior completed a 70-yard, six-play drive in 41 seconds with a 24-yard pass to Alvin Harper with 8:53 left for a 24-17 score.

After Colorado answered with a 78-yard breakaway touchdown on a pitchout to tailback Mike Pritchard for a

Dale Carter (18) celebrates after a key defensive play.

31-17 lead with 7:11 left in the game, Kelly wasn't stymied.

He directed an 87-yard, seven-play drive to Carl Pickens for the touchdown with 5:36 remaining. Colorado's lead was narrowed to 31-24.

The Vols' drive that tied the score at 31-31 was a 74-yard, 11-play jaunt in one minute 44 seconds. A 29-yard throw to Pickens was the big gainer. Webb then burst through for 4 yards for the touchdown with 2:25 left.

Kelly completed 33 of 55 passes for a career-best of 368 yards which set school records for completions and attempts.

Pritchard finished with 217 yards on 20 carries and scored two touchdowns.

A pack of Vols huddle together after the 31-31 tie with Colorado.

Majors Defends Decision

BY BOBBY HALL
The Commercial Appeal

ANAHEIM

Tennessee coach Johnny Majors said emphatically: "I made the decision."

It was the decision that meant the first Disneyland Pigskin Classic ended in a tie, 31-31.

Greg Burke's extra-point kick with 2:25 remaining pulled the Vols even with Colorado and that's the way the score remained.

"No. 1, I made the decision because I wanted to make it," Majors said. "No. 2, I thought we would get the ball back. No. 3, I thought we would bring the ball upfield when we got it back."

All those things happened.

"We just ran out of a couple of ticks," Majors said.

The game ended with UT at Colorado's 16-yard line.

Colorado coach Bill McCartney said, "I thought they were going for two. But I can understand the rationale not to."

It was left to Majors to explain the rationale.

"The decision is always a great decision; people always like to second guess it," Majors said. "But unless you are going for a championship at that time, a tie is a lot better than a loss. I'll stick to that a long, long time."

Explosive Vols Devour Gators

By Bobby Hall
The Commercial Appeal

KNOXVILLE, Oct. 13, 1990

| Florida | 0 | 3 | 0 | 0 | – | 3 |
| Tennessee | 0 | 7 | 28 | 10 | – | 45 |

A homecoming football game tonight that the University of Tennessee won't soon forget was one the University of Florida won't care to remember.

In a stunning display of explosiveness, the fifth-ranked Vols staked a bid for No. 1 by crushing the No. 9-ranked Gators, 45-3, before 96,874 in Neyland Stadium.

"We had a lot to prove," said Vols safety Dale Carter, who began the proof with a 91-yard return of the second half kickoff for a touchdown.

Before the third quarter was finished, the steam-rolling Vols had scored 28 points, extending a 7-3 half-time lead to 35-3.

"I can't remember a game when the situation changed more from the first half to the second half ... at least I can't think of one in my 24 years as a head coach," said UT coach Johnny Majors.

The victory left Tennessee (4-0-2, 2-0-1 in the SEC)

Roland Poles (42) looks for a hole in the Florida defensive wall.

Alvin Harper celebrates one of the Vols' many touchdowns.

tied atop the Southeastern Conference with Auburn. Florida fell to 5-1 and 3-1 in the SEC.

Tennessee's potent offense, led by tailback Tony Thompson's 103 yards on 18 carries, dominated in total yardage, 365-194. The Vols rushed for 240 yards against a Gator defense that came into the game as the SEC leader in rushing defense, allowing 79.4 yards, and in scoring, yielding 10.4 points per game.

The Vols defense harassed the Gators for five interceptions and three fumble recoveries. Carter got two of the interceptions. Freshman linebacker Reggie Ingram of Whitehaven recovered a fumble and returned an interception 22 yards for a touchdown.

"I saw the ball in the air and I always remembered how Coach Majors always says it's easier to catch it than drop it," Ingram said. "I caught it and took off."

Ingram's romp made the score 35-3.

Todd Kelly (58) enjoys a sack of Florida quarterback Shane Matthews.

TOP: Shon Walker (45) returns a Gator interception.

LEFT: Greg Amsler (47) tries to outrun a Florida defender to the corner.

"It was fairly close for a half, but things got out of hand fast," said Gator coach Steve Spurrier.

It was Majors' first victory against Florida in four tries and broke a four-game Gator victory streak in the series.

The crowd was the second largest in UT history, topped only by 97,372 for the 1985 Vanderbilt game. Included were nine bowl scouts, including the Sugar, Orange and Cotton.

Carter's game-breaking return began with him grabbing the ball just inside the right sideline. He quick-stepped up the sideline, then veered to his left with Gators diving at his heels. He got the last block he needed from sophomore David Bennett of Germantown, and suddenly Tennessee led, 14-3.

"They (Gators) had me two or three times by the arm, but an arm tackle won't bring me down,"

Clemons McCrosky cuts back against the Gator defense.

Tony Thompson (24) rushed for 108 yards on 18 carries.

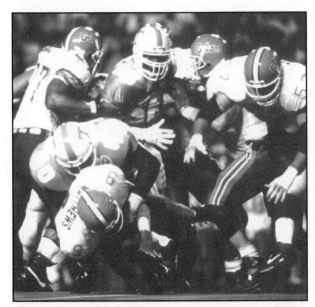

Florida quarterback Shane Matthews gets sacked again by the Vol defense.

Carter said. "There was a big hole, so I went through it."

After the kickoff return, the Vols drove 68 yards in 10 plays with Thompson, a senior from Frostproof, Fla., scoring a 13-yard run for a 21-3 lead. Then came some trickery — a 47-yard TD pass, thrown by tight end Von Reeves to flanker Carl Pickens. Reeves took a handoff then fired.

"I still had my glove on," said the 6-2, 234-pound Reeves, a former high school quarterback who now wears protective blocking gloves. "I figured if I took one of my gloves off, they would know something was up."

Carter's second interception set up a 36-yard field goal by Greg Burke with 11:58 remaining to increase the Vols' lead to 38-3. Three minutes later, after a fumble recovery by Ingram, the Vols made it 45-3 on a 1-yard run by quarterback Sterling Henton.

Tennessee Rallies Past Tough Cavaliers

BY BOBBY HALL
The Commercial Appeal

NEW ORLEANS, Jan. 1, 1991

The longest season in major college football ended tonight just like it began for the University of Tennessee — with a frantic comeback.

But this result was sweeter. The thundering rally by UT delivered a 23-22 victory over Virginia in the USF&G Sugar Bowl in the Louisiana Superdome.

A one-yard dive with 31 seconds left by senior tailback Tony Thompson, the Vols' captain, was good for the touchdown that saved No. 10 Tennessee in this 57th Sugar Bowl.

The TD capped a 79-yard drive that began with 2:24 remaining and included key yardage on powerful running and screen passes to fullback Greg Amsler.

The Vols, who twice rallied from two-touchdown deficits to tie Colorado, 31-31, Aug. 26 in the season opener, were down, 16-0, 16-3, and 19-10, before escaping.

Virginia quarterback Shawn Moore looks for an open receiver downfield.

Virginia	9	7	0	6	–	22
Tennessee	0	0	3	20	–	23

"Just another normal night at the office," Vols coach Johnny Majors said with a laugh. "It was a terrific comeback. Virginia did a fantastic job and played the heck out of us."

A crowd of 75,132, including about one-third of that total wearing UT orange, turned the Superdome into a din of celebration as the Vols finished with a 9-2-2 record.

Virginia, a five-point underdog and concerned because quarterback Shawn Moore was limited because of a thumb injury, dropped to 8-4.

But the Cavs, who once were No. 1 this season before losing three of their final four regular-season games, made the Vols work for everything.

Tennessee, the Southeastern Conference champion, was led by quarterback Andy Kelly and tailback Thompson.

The game-winning drive began with 2:24 remaining from the Vols' 21 with Kelly completing seven passes. Kelly finished with 24 completions in 35 attempts for 273 yards and one touchdown.

Kelly was named the winner of The Miller-Digby Award for the game's outstanding player.

"This by far was our best comeback because we came back and won ... against Colorado we didn't," Kelly said. "I thought we could keep moving the ball using the short stuff (passes), and we had enough time to do that on the final drive."

Thompson rushed for 151 yards and two TDs on 25 carries.

By halftime the Vols, and their fans, appeared stunned. For the first time all season, UT failed to score in a half.

Instead, the Vols, who were second nationally in turnover ratio for the season, turned the ball over three times, and missed a field goal attempt in the first 30 minutes.

"I was pretty darn upset at halftime," Majors said.

Virginia, making only its fourth bowl appearance in school history, wasn't bothered by the big-time bowl spotlight.

"They just made the big plays in the second half and we didn't," said Virginia coach George Welsh.

Floyd Miley (22) hurdles a teammate while chasing down a Virginia halfback.

Vols Go Sweetly into a Scary Night

BY AL DUNNING
The Commercial Appeal

NEW ORLEANS

Ever wonder what those letters stand for in front of the USF&G Sugar Bowl?

For more than 59 minutes of Sugar Bowl frustration tonight, those letters meant Ugly, Sad, Futile & Godawful to the University of Tennessee football team.

But thanks to a gutty comeback in a fitful finish, make it read Utterly Stupendous Finish & Gala.

Tennessee 23, Virginia 22.

Other bowls might have meant more Tuesday, but none was more nerve-shredding.

Tennessee's improbable victory at the end of a 9-2-2 season was almost a suicide, aided and abetted by an 8-4 Virginia team that flashed samples of the pizazz that earned them the No. 1 national ranking briefly in mid-October.

To the dismay of Big Orange rooters dominating the crowd of 75,132, the Vols looked for most of the night like the world's most overrated five-point favorites.

How did the Volunteers shoot themselves in the feet? Let us count the ways:

■ On their five possessions in the first half, the Vols lost the ball once on a fumble and twice on pass interceptions, punted the ball once for 13 yards and missed a 46-yard field goal attempt. The defense didn't fare much better. Fact is, if Virginia's Moore had been able to throw deep, it might have been 116-0 at half.

■ In the second half, the Vols drew a 15-yard penalty for running into a guy trying to fair-catch a punt. Later they ran into Virginia's punter, which allowed Virginia to keep the ball on a drive that produced a field goal and a 19-10 Wahoo lead.

It was such a lousy night for Tennessee that not even Elvis Presley got any respect.

Tennessee	0	14	7	14	– 35
Notre Dame	21	10	3	0	– 34

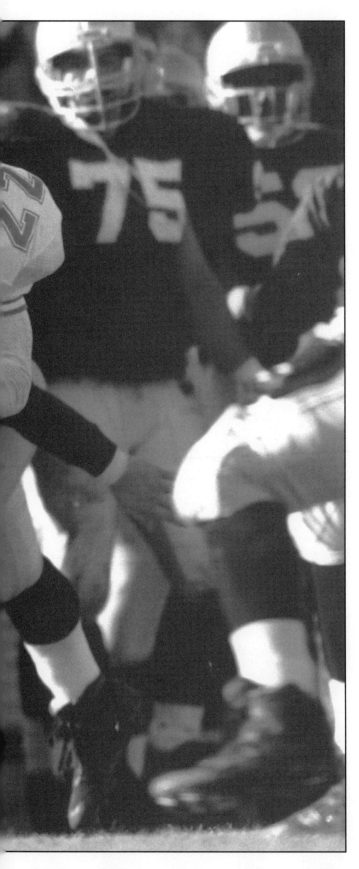

Vols Rally & Blocked Kicks Rock Irish

BY BOBBY HALL
The Commercial Appeal

SOUTH BEND, Ind., Nov. 9, 1991

The luck of the Irish ran out late today at Notre Dame Stadium, and the echoes that lingered into the cold night were of *Rocky Top*.

The Tennessee Volunteers — as happy as frolicking leprechauns — loved it.

The 13th-ranked Vols emerged a 35-34 winner when Notre Dame's 27-yard field goal attempt on the last play of the football game bounced off a UT player's buttock and sailed wide right.

"When I go home, my mom teases me about my big behind," said Jeremy Lincoln, the diving Vols cornerback whose hip deflected Rob Leonard's field goal try. "Today, it (Lincoln's posterior) paid off for us."

The loss probably ended fifth-ranked Notre Dame's dream for another national championship. The Fighting Irish fell to 8-2, losing for the first time since a 24-14 defeat at Michigan in their second game. The defeat was especially bitter because Notre Dame blew a 31-14 halftime lead.

In the second quarter, Floyd Miley (22) returned a blocked field goal 85 yards for a touchdown.

"I can't see anything positive about this," said Irish tailback Tony Brooks, who rushed for 126 yards and one touchdown.

It was the 300th game for Notre Dame at the famed stadium. The loss, only the Irish's third at home in the last 29 games, came before a chilled capacity crowd of 59,075.

The Vols (6-2) put the guardian ghosts of Notre Dame's proud legacy to sleep early, then struck while they dozed. UT self-destructed with first-half turnovers and trailed, 21-0, after the first quarter, and 31-7 late in the second period.

But Tennessee, which lost to Notre Dame, 34-29, in the final seconds last year at Knoxville, outscored the Irish in the second half, 21-3.

"There was never a sense of panic in the huddle," said Vols quarterback Andy Kelly, who triggered UT's conversion of three fourth-down plays in the second half. "We knew we had time."

UT will play host to Ole Miss in a Southeastern Conference game next Saturday. Notre Dame will play at Penn State.

Kelly threw for 259 yards and three TDs, becoming UT's all-time passing yardage leader. Freshman tailback Aaron Hayden rushed for 82 yards and one TD and scored on a 26-yard pass from Kelly with 4:03 to play, tying the game, 34-34.

John Becksvoort converted the decisive extra-point kick.

The Vols had three turnovers in the first 30 minutes, helping Notre Dame lead, 31-14.

A fumbled punt by UT's Dale Carter after Notre Dame's first series allowed the Irish to keep the ball, and the result was a 47-yard, five-play TD drive. Brooks scored on a 12-yard run for a 7-0 lead.

Carter ran back the ensuing kickoff back 62 yards, and the Vols came out throwing — something many UT fans demanded after losses to Florida and Alabama. The strategy backfired, however.

On first down, Kelly overthrew a receiver badly, and on the next play Kelly's underthrown pass was intercepted by cornerback Tom Carter and returned 79 yards for a TD.

Late in the first period, Notre Dame stretched its lead to 21-0 with a 94-yard, 11-play drive that quarterback Rick Mirer finished with a 10-yard TD run.

The Vols used a nine-play, 65-yard march to make the score 21-7 early in the second quarter. Kelly passed 21 yards to flanker Cory Fleming for the touchdown.

Notre Dame responded with Craig Hentrich's 24-

UT defensive back Dale Carter misses a tackle on Irish quarterback Rick Mirer's 10-yard, first-quarter touchdown run.

Vol defensive lineman Chuck Smith sacks the Irish quarterback.

pass from Kelly and fumbled on the hit by safety Willie Clark; linebacker Greg Davis recovered.

The Irish drove 59 yards in eight plays to score, with fullback Jerome Bettis crashing over from the 2 for his 17th touchdown of the season and a 31-7 lead.

Desperate for points, UT attempted to convert a fourth and 1 from its 45-yard line and failed with 67 seconds left in the half. The break for Notre Dame, however, turned into disaster.

Hentrich's 32-yard field goal attempt was blocked by Vols linebacker Darryl Hardy. Cornerback Floyd Miley picked up the ball and ran 85 yards for a TD, pulling UT to 31-14. Hentrich was caught in a tangle of blockers on the runback and sustained a knee injury.

UT drove 71 yards in 11 plays for a TD midway through the third period, making it 31-21. Kelly passed 4 yards to tight end Von Reeves for the TD. Hentrich returned to the game to kick a 28-yard field goal to give the Irish a 34-21 lead, but he reinjured his knee on the ensuing kickoff.

Carter's interception at the Irish 45 with 6:40 left set up the Vols' final scoring chance. Kelly then hit Hayden on a screen pass for the 26-yard TD.

Notre Dame roared back on its final drive, reaching the Vols' 9. With four seconds left and facing a fourth-and-3 situation, Leonard, a walk-on sophomore, was sent in to kick because of Hentrich's injury.

"A man came from the outside and got a piece of it," Leonard said. "The ball went about a yard and a half to the right."

The Vols and about 5,000 UT fans went crazy.

yard field goal, then took advantage of another UT turnover to start a TD drive that produced a 31-7 lead. The turnover came when Fleming caught a 15-yard

A Miracle Gets Away from Irish

By Al Dunning
The Commercial Appeal

SOUTH BEND, Ind.

Tennessee's 35-34 comeback win in South Bend was one of its greatest ever.

For the first 54 years, 10 months and 3 days of Lou Holtz's life, things went reasonably well. Then came today.

Minutes after Tennessee pulled the slickest escape this side of Houdini and benumbed Notre Dame, 35-34, someone asked the Irish coach if this was the most disappointing day in his six seasons at Notre Dame.

"It's the most disappointing day of my life," Holtz replied. "I've been in this game a long time, and this is as tough a loss as I've ever been associated with — ever."

Hey, Lou, now you know how all those other guys feel. What befell the Irish today was the kind of disaster that has been happening to visiting teams at Notre Dame for 105 years.

In a stadium full of legends, Tennessee wrote a storybook classic of its own Saturday. Behind, 14-0, before the game was four minutes old, the Vols spotted Notre Dame a 31-7 lead in the second quarter ... what looked hopeless for Tennessee at that point began to look even worse when Notre Dame rolled to a first and goal at the Vols' 9-yard line just before halftime.

That's where the Irish ran out of shamrocks. Tennessee's Darryl Hardy blocked a field goal attempt, teammate Floyd Miley ran it back 85 yards for a touchdown, and Tennessee still had vital signs at halftime, down 31-14.

Tennessee coach Johnny Majors called the TD off the blocked kick "one of the greatest plays any football team has ever had."

Well, at least until the Volunteers pulled another improbable one on the last play of the game.

Tennessee capped its thunderous rally with a 26-yard TD pass from Andy Kelly to Aaron Hayden at 4:03 left in the game. John Becksvoort's extra point kick nudged the Vols ahead, 35-34 ... and here came Notre Dame, unleashing the kind of inspired drive that makes Irish football history read like science fiction.

Only this time, the leprechauns defected. With regular placekicker Craig Hentrich sidelined by a strained knee suffered when the Vols blocked his first-half field goal attempt, Notre Dame sent in walk-on sophomore kicker Rob Leonard to attempt a 27-yard field goal on the game's last play.

Slightly low snap, slightly low kick. The ball nicked the backside of diving UT rusher Jeremy Lincoln and deflected ever-so-slightly wide right.

"That's what hurts; having a chance and not getting it done," Holtz said, shaking his head like a fighter trying to clear the cobwebs. "You're way ahead, they come back, you're losing the ballgame and boom! You come down and have a chance and you don't get it."

Although he clearly was less than pleased with his backup placekicker ("You got to be able to get the ball up," Holtz said), Holtz thought Notre Dame's defense shared the rap for losing a game that appeared to be safely in the sack.

"Whether you have a big enough lead or not depends on how well you're playing defense," he said. "I didn't see us playing much defense the second half."

From the other side of Notre Dame Stadium, the world looked infinitely prettier.

That's because the setting was so special, here in one of the shrines of college football.

"I can't describe in words the meaning of this win and the way it happened," Majors said. "I don't know that we've had a more important or a bigger comeback over a significant opponent in our university's history.

"When you consider the ranking of the opponent (Notre Dame was No. 5) and the significance of where we played ... well, it was special."

The victory raised No. 13 Tennessee's record to 6-2. Notre Dame dropped to 8-2 ... and for Holtz, it was a deep, deep plunge.

"I don't know where we go from here, I really don't," he said. "You just sit there and try to keep your faith in God.

"Postseason? I have no idea," Holtz said. "I don't care. I have absolutely no interest in that right now."

Shuler-led 80-yard March Finishes 'Dawgs

BY RON HIGGINS
The Commercial Appeal

ATHENS, Ga., Sept. 12, 1992

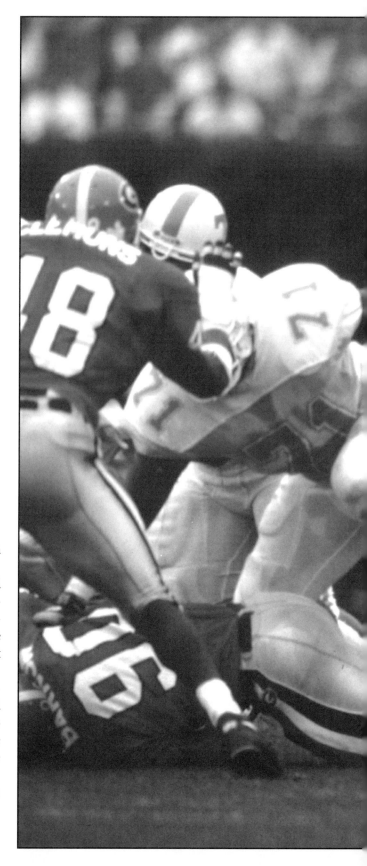

It can be safely assumed that Heath Shuler has won Tennessee's quarterbacking job.

The clincher in his resume was an 80-yard game-winning drive capped by a 3-yard touchdown keeper with 50 seconds left to propel the 20th-ranked Volunteers to a 34-31 Southeastern Conference football victory over 14th-ranked Georgia today at Samford Stadium.

With a crowd of 85,434 screaming as loudly as possible, Shuler, a sophomore starting just his second game, completed a 22-yard, fourth-and-14 pass to Bartlett's Ronald Davis at the Georgia 18. It kept the drive alive with just under two minutes left. Three plays later, Shuler scored.

Georgia's last chance died with 14 seconds left when

Aaron Hayden (24) watches as the huge running lane opens before him.

Tennessee	6	7	7	14	–	34
Georgia	3	14	0	14	–	31

Backup quarterback Jerry Colquitt is sacked by a Bulldog pass rusher.

receiver Andre Hastings had the ball stripped by Tennessee's George Kidd. Linebacker Reggie Ingram of Memphis Whitehaven recovered at the Tennessee 34.

The upset gave the Vols a 2-0 overall record and gave them a share of the SEC's Eastern Division lead with Florida at 1-0. The Gators, victors over Kentucky today, play at Tennessee next Saturday. The Bulldogs are 1-1 overall and 1-1 in the SEC.

The win was also the second for Tennessee interim coach Phillip Fulmer, subbing for Johnny Majors, who is recovering from heart surgery. After a midfield postgame handshake with 'Dawgs coach Ray Goff, Fulmer jumped up and down like a schoolboy and leaped into the arms of offensive linemen Brian Spivey and David Bell.

"We have a million miles to go," Fulmer said, "We gave up too many big plays, but we played with an air of confidence. This was truly a team win." Fulmer beamed over players who played beyond their inexperience. Shuler was the prime example as he stepped in the huddle with six minutes left, the Vols trailing, 31-27, and with three-fourths of the field to cover.

"We had just gone 80 yards on our previous scoring drive, so we were all confident we could go the dis-

The Vols were unable to slow down Garrison Hearst, who had 161 yards rushing on 20 attempts.

Heath Shuler passed for 233 yards and ran for two touchdowns in his second starting assignment.

David Bennett's shoestring tackle pulls down a Bulldog.

James Stewart hurdles the middle of the Georgia defense.

tance," said Shuler, who had 233 of Tennessee's 382 yards total offense and scored twice himself. "We knew we could get it done."

Shuler's brilliant offensive direction brought Tennessee from a 17-13 halftime deficit to a 27-17 lead with 12:36 left to play.

Drives of 50 and 80 yards ended with Tennessee touchdowns on runs of 2 and 4 yards by fullback Mario Brunson and Shuler, respectively.

The latter drive was kept alive by Shuler's 44-yard run on the last play of the third period, keeping the ball on what he called "part quarterback draw, option."

Georgia was far from done because of quarterback Eric Zeier and running back Garrison Hearst. Zeier threw for 354 yards and one TD, and Hearst scored twice in the fourth quarter on runs of 64 yards at 12:01 and 17 yards at 6:00. Hearst finished with 161 yards on 20 carries.

The last touchdown gave Georgia its four-point lead that it thought it could hold. But in the end, Bulldogs coach Goff seemed shocked that his team folded in the clutch.

"This hurts; I don't think I've ever had one hurt as bad as this," Goff said.

While Georgia rolled up 569 yards the Vols caused four fumbles and picked off two passes.

Georgia's fumbling problems were caused by shoddy ball-carrying and some solid hits by the Volunteers.

"We noticed on film from their game against South Carolina last week how Georgia running backs kind of carried the ball out loose away from their bodies," Ingram said. "Everytime we hit them, we tried to strip them."

That's precisely how the game started when Georgia's Ha'son Graham fumbled the opening kickoff to set up a quick Tennessee field goal.

Another fumble, an interception, a missed field goal, 30 penalty yards and three UT sacks stopped the Bulldogs from doing major damage in the first half.

Shuler Throws TD, Runs for 2 More to Drop Gators

BY RON HIGGINS
The Commercial Appeal

KNOXVILLE, Sept. 19, 1992

M other Nature provided thunder and a first-class rainstorm at Neyland Stadium today.

No. 14-ranked Tennessee added the lightning, and No. 4-ranked Florida felt the shock of a 31-14 Big Orange gullywasher that boosted the Vols to the top of Southeastern Conference's Eastern Division.

The Vols took a 17-7 halftime lead, then pushed the margin to 31-7 in a driving rainstorm that lasted from 9 minutes left in the third quarter to 10 minutes left to play. Tennessee (3-0 overall, 2-0 in the SEC), which plays Cincinnati next, dominated Florida (1-1, 1-1 in the SEC) and snapped the Gators' 11-game SEC winning streak.

From Vols sophomore quarterback Heath Shuler, who threw for a touchdown and ran for two more

Charlie Garner (30) rumbles for yardage in the Florida secondary.

Florida	0	7	0	7	–	14
Tennessee	7	10	7	7	–	31

scores, to a fierce attacking defense that limited Florida senior quarterback Shane Matthews to less than 200 yards passing for the first time in 19 games, it was all Tennessee.

"Coming into the season, people were expecting us to win five or six games," said Tennessee junior tailback Charlie Garner, who ran for a team-high 82 yards on 16 carries. "We're letting people know that we're for real."

Perhaps the only person who left the stadium without illusions of grandeur was Tennessee interim coach Phillip Fulmer. He could have gloated about back-to-back wins over ranked teams — the Vols beat 14th-ranked Georgia last Saturday, 34-31 — but he didn't.

"I don't want anybody making reservations for Birmingham or New Orleans," said Fulmer, referring to the sites of the SEC championship game and the Sugar Bowl, respectively.

The third-largest crowd in Neyland Stadium history, 97,137, watched the Vols, who outgained the high-octane Gators, 344-278, make a load of big plays. They ranged from a blocked punt to stopping a fake punt to Shuler's 66-yard touchdown pass, caught by sophomore running back Mose Phillips, for a 24-7

Mario Brunson (44) ran like a bulldozer against Florida.

Tennessee halfback James Stewart savors his trip to the Florida end zone.

lead late in the third quarter.

To Florida coach Steve Spurrier, whose two SEC losses in 16 conference games have been to Tennessee, the defeat looked a lot like the Gators' 45-3 loss to the Vols here two years ago.

"Like two years ago, we were beaten in every aspect of the game," Spurrier said.

A supreme effort from the Vols' beleaguered defense, which gave up 569 yards to Georgia, made a huge difference.

The Vols knocked Florida star tailback Errict Rhett, the SEC's leading rusher, out for most of the game with an ankle injury sustained on his second carry of the afternoon. He finished with 34 yards on 11 carries.

Matthews — a senior Heisman Trophy candidate — completed just 12-of-23 passes for 149 yards.

"Matthews probably didn't expect this," said UT senior defensive end Todd Kelly, who had one sack

Vols quarterback Heath Shuler threw for a touchdown and ran for two more.

Charlie Garner (30) darts through a large opening in the Florida secondary.

and put constant pressure on Matthews. "He probably looked at our Georgia film and thought he was going to throw for 500 yards against us."

Tennessee's Tracy Smith blocked a Shayne Edge punt and it took the Vols two plays to score their opening TD — an 11-yard Shuler keeper with 1:28 left in the first quarter.

Tennessee's most important drive of the game may have been after Florida sliced the Vols' cushion to 14-7 on Matthews' 10-yard scoring strike to Aubrey Hill with 2:50 left in the first half.

Keyed by Garner's stop-and-start 31-yard run, Tennessee got a 35-yard John Becksvoort field goal with nine seconds left.

The roof and the sky fell in on Florida in the third quarter. While the Gators managed a paltry 11

Charlie Garner and Heath Shuler at the point of attack.

yards in the quarter, Tennessee broke the game open on a calculated gamble by the braintrust of Fulmer and quarterbacks coach David Cutcliffe.

On third and 5 at the Tennessee 34-yard line, the Vols called a waggle pass that had Shuler faking a handoff left and rolling right. Receiver Craig Faulkner ran deep to clear the side and Phillips ran past a blitzing linebacker. He caught Shuler's short pass, got key blocks from Faulkner and Robert Todd of Germantown High and navigated his way through the rain to score the first TD of his career with 2:49 left in the third quarter.

"The pass surprised me as much as it surprised them," Phillips said. "I was surprised to be that open."

Just one more shock in an electrifying day for Tennessee.

UT Pass Rush, Rain Swamp Matthews, Gators

By Ron Higgins
The Commercial Appeal

KNOXVILLE

Tennessee's defensive game plan against Florida today provided an anatomy lesson — take care of Gators running back Errict Rhett's ankle and quarterback Shane Matthews' head.

A knifing tackle by Tennessee's J.J. McCleskey sprained Rhett's ankle on the second play of the game. Then, a first-half sack of Matthews by Tennessee's Todd Kelly had him looking over his shoulder the rest of the day.

By the time a second-half rain drenched Neyland Stadium, the Gators were on their way to drowning themselves in offensive sorrow, contributing to Tennessee's 31-14 Southeastern Conference football upset.

Without Rhett — the SEC's leading rusher — in the Gators' backfield, the Vols went after Matthews and limited the Heisman Trophy candidate to 149 passing yards.

No one was happier to see such a performance than Tennessee defensive coordinator Larry Marmie, whose defense gave up 569 yards to Georgia the previous week in UT's 34-31 victory. Florida gained just 278 yards, well under the average of 460.7 yards per game during Florida's previous 24 games with Steve Spurrier as the Gators' coach.

"There are certain days when you feel like you can control the line of scrimmage and this was one of them," Marmie said. "Last week was not one of them."

After Georgia rolled for the third highest total yards against the Vols in school history, the UT defense went back to the practice field.

"Against Georgia, we missed a lot of tackles and overran the ball a lot," Kelly said.

There were other problem areas also, said defensive tackle J. J. Surlas.

"We may not have been in great physical condition against Georgia, so we worked a lot on conditioning," said Surlas. "That helped, plus the fact we were able to play three-deep at a lot of positions today. Florida's line got kind of tired."

Without Rhett, Tennessee was able to worry less about Florida's favorite running play — Rhett on a draw cutting back against the grain. The Vols were able to go after Matthews, who was being protected by a line that entered the season a week ago against Kentucky with just 12 combined career starts.

"When we saw Rhett go to the sideline and get treated by the trainer, we got pumped up," Kelly said. "Then, we got into Matthews' head. He got frustrated and he started worrying about me. Their freshman tackle (Reggie Green) even jumped offsides twice worrying about me."

Matthews said he missed having Rhett, who ran for a career-high 193 yards in Florida's 35-19 season-opening victory over Kentucky last week.

"It hurts us anytime we don't have Errict in the game," Matthews said. "He must have really been hurting because he wants to play every down of every game."

Spurrier said Matthews didn't have time to make decisions.

"We spread our offense out at the end of the first half and scored," Spurrier said. "But in the second half over the next two or three possessions, Shane didn't have time. Credit Tennessee for an outstanding pass rush. They got to us when they needed to get to us."

When it started pouring during the third quarter with Tennessee leading, 17-7, no one was smiling wider than drenched UT coach Phillip Fulmer.

"We were up 10 points on a throwing team, so the rain was welcome," Fulmer said. "I don't think the Good Lord cares who wins football games — He's got more important things to worry about. But the timing of the rain was very good."

Fulmer said the rain didn't bother him, but the Gatorade shower from his players did. "I really could have done without the Gatorade. It was freezing."

Volunteer Juggernaut Clobbers Vanderbilt

BY THOMAS HARDING
The Commercial Appeal

NASHVILLE, Nov. 26, 1994

Charlie Garner (30) returns an interception of a Vanderbilt pass.

Tennessee running back James (Little Man) Stewart stayed up all Friday night, expecting a rough Saturday afternoon at Vanderbilt Stadium.

Turned out there was no point losing sleep.

Stewart rushed for 122 yards to become the school's career rushing leader and Tennessee set a school record with 665 yards while beating Vanderbilt, 65-0, in the Southeastern Conference regular-season football finale for both teams before 38,816.

Stewart, who finishes with 2,890 career regular-season rushing yards, surpassing Johnnie Jones' 2,852 yards in 1981-84, never dreamed of such an outcome.

"Who would've?" said Stewart, who has gained 1,028 yards this season. "They're an improved Vanderbilt team. We knew they were going to come in and play us hard.

"Everybody was on the same page. Everything just worked out."

Tennessee (7-4, 5-3 in the SEC) now must wait to find where it will play in the postseason.

The Mazda Gator Bowl has the third choice of SEC teams in college football's bowl coalition and could pick either the Vols or Mississippi State (8-3, 5-3 in the SEC). The Gator Bowl committee will meet Monday. The team that doesn't go to the Gator Bowl on Dec. 30 in Gainesville, Fla., will likely go to the Peach Bowl Jan. 1 in Atlanta.

Tennessee finished the regular season by outscoring Kentucky and Vanderbilt by a combined 124-0.

"I think it's obvious our football team was ready to play," Tennessee coach Phillip Fulmer said. "We've improved every week for the last five or six weeks."

Tennessee	7	31	20	7	- 65
Vanderbilt	0	0	0	0	- 0

Vol lineman Shane Bonham sacks the Vandy quarterback.

ning by racing to a 37-0 halftime lead.

To compound the insult, the Vols outrushed the Commodores, 406-129, to wrest away the rushing title with a 231.2-yard average per game. Vandy entered leading the league, 22.7 yards per game ahead of Tennessee, but finished the season with a 226.6 average.

"They were hyped up, but I really didn't think they were as good as people had thought," Tennessee guard Kevin Mays said.

"I read some headlines this morning and they tried to say Vanderbilt is an even match with Tennessee. Vanderbilt is Vanderbilt and Tennessee is Tennessee."

About the only downer for the Vols was seeing running back Aaron Hayden leave the game with two broken bones in his right leg with 30 seconds left in the first half. Hayden had rushed for 77 yards and needed 29 more to move into fifth on UT's career rushing list and surpass Charlie Garner, now with the Philadelphia Eagles. Hayden finished his career with 2,061.

Tennessee scored on five of its seven first-half possessions and scored just about any possible way.

The Vols' first drive was all Stewart — three carries for 48 yards, including a 40-yarder for a touchdown and a 7-0 lead.

Tennessee kicker John Becksvoort later extended his consecutive extra points string to an NCAA-record 161.

Wide receiver Nilo Silvan circled right end for an 8-yard touchdown run on a reverse for a 14-0 lead with 14:48 left in the second quarter.

One play after Stewart broke the school career rushing record with a 9-yard run, freshman backup quarterback Brandon Stewart completed his first collegiate touchdown pass — a 21-yarder to Billy Williams.

Vanderbilt (5-6, 2-6 in the SEC) entered with hopes of finishing with a winning season and earning its first bowl bid since 1982, and of winning the SEC team rushing title.

It achieved none of them. Instead, it was Vanderbilt's worst loss since a 71-0 loss to Alabama in 1945. Tennessee has built a greater victory margin just twice — 73-0 over Carson-Newman in 1929 and 68-0 over Tennessee Tech in 1951.

"We got what we deserved today," Commodores coach Gerry DiNardo said. "We have to realize that when they have an opportunity they had to make the best of it."

Tennessee dashed the Commodores' hopes of win-

Volunteers Finally Get Tide Off Their Back

BY RON HIGGINS
The Commercial Appeal

BIRMINGHAM, Oct. 14, 1995

This news flash just in: Tennessee Gov. Don Sundquist has declared Monday as "Tennessee Football Day." But the good governor probably doesn't need to do anything such as give the Vols a key to the state capitol.

After all, the No. 6 Vols already got the key they needed tonight — how to get into No. 12 Alabama's end zone quite often — as Tennessee trounced the Crimson Tide, 41-14, and ended a nine-year winless streak against Alabama before a Legion Field crowd of 83,091.

The Vols jumped to a 21-0 first-quarter lead and the Tide had few answers for Tennessee sophomore quarterback Peyton Manning. He had his fourth 300-yard passing game in the last six contests, throwing for 301 yards, three touchdowns and running for another score.

Manning's 80-yard touchdown pass to wide receiver

Vol quarterback Peyton Manning passed for 301 yards and three touchdowns and ran for another score.

Tennessee	21	7	7	6 –	41
Alabama	0	7	7	0 –	14

Joey Kent on Tennessee's first offensive play set the tone for what became an exorcism of almost a decade of frustration. Overcome with the emotion of breaking a nine-game winless streak against the Tide (4-2, 2-2 in the SEC), the Vols rushed to their cheering section at game's end while the band played Rocky Top loud enough to be heard back in Knoxville. In the Tennessee dressing room, players and coaches were treated to victory cigars which has been an Alabama custom when it has beaten the Vols.

"I don't even know what to say," said Tennessee coach Phillip Fulmer, whose team improved to 6-1 overall and 4-1 in the SEC heading into its first open date of the season.

"I certainly hadn't anticipated coming out and leading 21-0. But when you have a talent like Peyton Manning, a great group of receivers and a line that can protect, something like that can happen."

With Manning doing his usual amazing job of finding the soft spots in defense, Tennessee totaled 496 yards offense against the SEC's top-rated defense. The Vols averaged 7.4 yards per snap with receivers Kent and Marcus Nash having 117 and 100 yards receiving, respectively, and running back Jay Graham running for 114 yards.

Alabama's first mistake was winning the coin toss and deferring its option to the second half, which meant that Tennessee's high-powered offense got first possession.

And it didn't last long — 14 seconds. That was long enough for Manning to take a look at the Tide's 3-3-5 defensive alignment, find a gap on the right side and slip an short pass to Kent, who zig-zagged 80 yards for a stunning touchdown. It only got better for the Vols as they scored on their next two possessions.

Manning zipped a perfectly-thrown third-down 25-yard scoring strike to Nash with 7:42 left, then followed that with 5:04 remaining using a deft bootleg 1-yard keeper that fooled Alabama so badly that Manning could have scored on crutches.

"It was a great feeling leading, 21-0, but we knew a big lead didn't mean much," Manning said. "We had a big lead when we lost at Florida a few weeks ago, and they came back in that game. At halftime, we said, 'Remember Florida. Let's go out. Defense don't give 'em anything. Offense no turnovers and let's run some clock. Let's put this game away.' And we did that."

Staring at a 21-0 deficit and believing his starting quarterback Brian Burgdorf was clearly rattled, Tide coach Gene Stallings yanked Burgdorf and

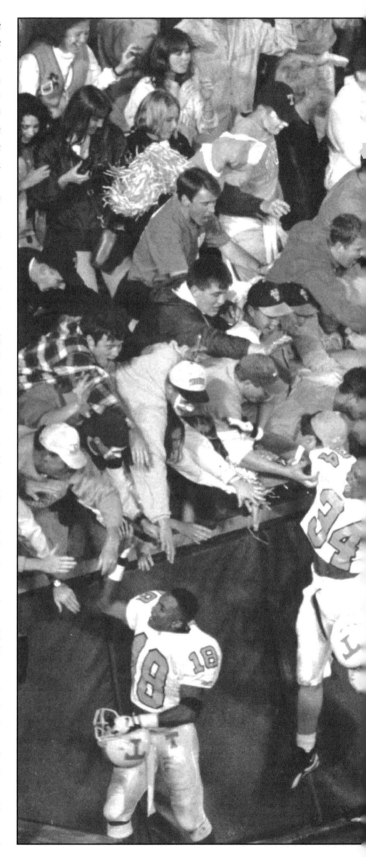

The Vol defense kept the pressure up on Alabama quarterback Brian Burgdorf.

inserted little-used Freddie Kitchens.

Kitchens twice helped cut the Vols' lead to 14 points at 21-7 with 6:10 left in the first half and 28-14 with 2:04 left in the third quarter. But his scrambling style also resulted in six sacks as the Tide barely broke 300 yards in total offense (303) and had five turnovers.

Each time Alabama cut the lead, Tennessee responded with touchdowns. The first was Manning's 30-yard TD to Nash on a crossing route through the heart of the Tide's troubled defense with 43 seconds left in the first half and a 28-7 halftime lead.

And on the Vols' first offensive play following Alabama's third-quarter TD, which cut UT's lead to two TDs, Manning recognized an Alabama blitz from the left side, handed the ball to Graham and watched him skirt right end on a career-long 75-yard touchdown run.

Tennessee led, 35-14, with 1:43 left in the third quarter, and the Crimson Tide were through for the night.

After the game, the Tennessee players celebrated with their fans in the end zone.

For Tennessee, Frustration's End Came Right Away

BY RON HIGGINS
The Commercial Appeal

BIRMINGHAM

All day in his hotel room, Tennessee offensive coordinator David Cutcliffe thought about what play he wanted to use as the Vols' opening salvo against Alabama.

Guess he picked the right one.

Quarterback Peyton Manning threw an 80-yard touchdown pass to Joey Kent 14 seconds into the game and Alabama was on its heels the rest of the night in a 41-14 Tennessee victory at Legion Field.

"I have lot of options I talk about and I pay attention to where we get the ball on the field," Cutcliffe said. "I played the game 100 times in my hotel, but I didn't decide what play to use until I saw where we had the ball."

Manning completed 20-of-29 passes for 301 yards, three touchdowns and was sacked just three times. He was the first quarterback to throw for more than 300 yards against Alabama since 1989 when Southern Mississippi's Brett Favre threw for 300 in a 37-14 loss to the Tide.

As he approached the line of scrimmage for his first snap of the game, Manning's eyes practically lit up.

"They subbed in with a nickel package (five defensive backs) and went with a cover three zone,"

Alabama backup quarterback Freddie Kitchens was unable to muster his team against the Vol defense.

Manning said. "I looked to the outside receiver and their defender buzzed out to pick him up. That left Joey on a clean release right down the middle and I hit him quick. Joey usually tells me during the game, 'Let's hook up.' This time, he told me before the game. I'm glad he did. We didn't waste much time."

Manning had so many pretty plays it was hard to count them all, but the one he'll remember for a while was his 1-yard bootleg touchdown keeper around left end for a 21-0 lead with 5:04 left in the first quarter. He faked to a diving Jay Graham and walked in untouched, running a play he had seen on film many times as a kid watching his father Archie execute the play as Ole Miss's star quarterback.

"We put that play in this week," Manning said. "As my dad says, you've got to have ice-water in your veins. I call the play and I kind of say I'm keeping it."

Late in the first half, after Alabama reduced Tennessee's lead to 21-7, Manning drove the Vols 72 yards in six plays and fired a 30-yard TD pass to Marcus Nash for a 28-7 lead with 42 seconds left before the break.

Manning slightly audibled on the play, but gave much of the credit to Nash.

"They were kind of doubling on Nash, but he beat the double coverage inside and got in the end zone," Manning said.

With an open date this week, Manning has time to revel in the victory. But he won't for too long.

"I've got a paper due for a class Wednesday," he said. "It will be nice that I'll be able to stay at the library until 10 p.m. each night instead of worrying about looking at game film."

Vols vs. Tide: End of the Line

1995: Tennessee 41, Alabama 14
1994: Alabama 17, Tennessee 13
1993: Alabama 17, Tennessee 17
1992: Alabama 17, Tennessee 10
1991: Alabama 24, Tennessee 19
1990: Alabama 9, Tennessee 6
1989: Alabama 47, Tennessee 30
1988: Alabama 28, Tennessee 20
1987: Alabama 41, Tennessee 22
1986: Alabama 56, Tennessee 28
1985: Tennessee 16, Alabama 14

Tennessee Defense Puts Squeeze on Ohio State

By Ron Higgins
The Commercial Appeal

ORLANDO, Jan. 1, 1996

| Ohio State | 7 | 0 | 0 | 7 | – | 14 |
| Tennessee | 0 | 7 | 7 | 6 | – | 20 |

To the year-long critics of Tennessee's defense, especially those who didn't sit through the pouring rain of Monday's 50th annual Florida Citrus Bowl, the Vols' defenders have a message:

Even if you didn't sit in the stands, you're all wet.

The Big Orange defense won the Vols' biggest game of the year, stopping Ohio State with a second-quarter goal-line stand and forcing three fourth-quarter fumbles as the No. 4 Vols held on for a 20-14 victory over the co-No. 4 Buckeyes.

Victory wasn't in hand before a soaked crowd of 70,797 until Tennessee cornerback DeRon Jenkins leveled Ohio State receiver Dimitrious Stanley, who fumbled with 57 seconds left. Tennessee linebacker

Ohio State quarterback Bobby Hoying is double-teamed by the Vol defense.

Craig King recovered at the Tennessee 38-yard line, clinching an 11-1 finish and the fifth 11-win season in Vols' history. Ohio State finished 11-2, losing its last two.

"As a defense, we just weren't going to be denied," said Vols' senior linebacker Scott Galyon, making six tackles and recovering the first of Ohio State's fourth-quarter fumbles. "We kept thinking, 'One more stop, one more stop.'"

Admittedly, the high-octane offenses of the Vols and the Buckeyes drowned somewhat in the rain that stopped just once, in the third quarter. The final statistics could hardly have been more even — Ohio State outgained Tennessee, 335-327, the Vols held a 30:39-29:21 edge in possession time and both teams lost the same amount of rushing yardage (29).

The teams matched in other individual weapons, even though the game's Most Valuable Player, Jay Graham of Tennessee, outrushed Ohio State Heisman Trophy winner Eddie George, 154-101, with each scoring once.

The difference was turnovers. Ohio State had four, Tennessee had one and the Vols made the two biggest offensive plays of the soggy afternoon.

Graham broke a simple draw play for a game-tying 69-yard touchdown run with 23 seconds left in the first half. Quarterback Peyton Manning's 47-yard scoring strike to Joey Kent with 13:22 left in the third quarter gave the Vols a 14-7 lead.

Ohio State pulled into a 14-14 tie on quarterback Bobby Hoying's 32-yard TD pass to tight end Rickey Dudley with 14:40 left, but the Vols responded with Jeff Hall field goals of 29 yards with 9:24 remaining and 25 yards with 2:06 left.

And the Vols' defense held on, forcing one last turnover to give Tennessee coach Phillip Fulmer his third bowl win in four tries.

"The bottom line for us was the spirit of this team," Fulmer said. "We showed character and the kids got it done."

The Vols, trailing 7-0, were on the verge of going over the edge with 6:21 left in the first half.

Ohio State, primed at the Tennessee 24-yard line following Vols' tailback Eric Lane's fumble, ran George five straight times to the Vols' 2-yard line where the Buckeyes faced fourth and inches for a first down.

But against the nation's fifth-ranked offense, the Vols stuffed George for a 2-yard loss with linebacker Jesse Sanders submarining a blocker and tackle Bill Duff coming over the top. Amazingly, the Buckeyes' ran the play away from the side of Outland Trophy-winning lineman Orlando Pace.

"If we couldn't make six inches with a Heisman Trophy winner, then maybe we shouldn't deserve to win the game anyway," said miffed Ohio State coach John Cooper.

After an exchange of punts, the Vols got the ball back with 41 seconds left at the Tennessee 20-yard line. Fulmer acknowledged he was hoping to get the Vols into field goal position.

Graham got 11 yards on a draw play, being tripped by the last available tackler. He jumped to his feet chastising himself for not going all the way. Little did he know on the next play, he'd find the same hole, hop over a diving tackler, shake off another and sprint the distance for the TD that breathed life into the dying Vols.

Buckeye Heisman winner Eddie George looks in a pass.

Peyton Manning prepares to unload against the Buckeyes.

"Ohio State's defense did a good job of stunting and twisting into holes — they guessed a lot of plays right," Graham said. "That time, we caught them in a twist, (tight end) Scott Pfeiffer made the block and I was gone."

Tennessee's opening drive of the second half was kept alive by a roughing-the-punter penalty. The Vols took advantage immediately after the infraction with Manning throwing a wobbly TD bomb that Kent stopped and came back to grab over confused Ohio State defender Antoine Winfield.

Joey Kent scored on a 47-yard pass from Manning in the third quarter.

Volunteers' Big Plays Sink Buckeyes

BY RON HIGGINS
The Commercial Appeal

ORLANDO

It was the key play of the game for the Tennessee defense in the Vols' 20-14 Florida Citrus Bowl victory over Ohio State today.

But which play was it?

It could been Tennessee's Bill Duff throwing Heisman Trophy winner Eddie George of Ohio State for a 2-yard loss on fourth and 1 at the Tennessee 2 with 3:26 left in the second quarter.

It could have been the Vols' Leonard Little forcing fourth-quarter fumbles by George and by quarterback Bobby Hoying, the latter an errant option pitch on fourth and 1 at midfield with 5:07 left.

It could have been Tennessee's DeRon Jenkins slapping loose a fumble by Ohio State's Dimitrious Stanley to snuff the Buckeyes' last threat with 57 seconds left.

"Nobody thought we could hold an offense like Ohio State's to 14 points, but we were confident we could if everyone played to their capabilities," Jenkins said.

The Vols' defense was so effective that the Buckeyes rushed George just four times in the final quarter.

He just barely broke 101 yards for the day on 25 carries, struggling as the primary target of the Tennessee defenders.

"I expected all day to get hit like that," said George, whose longest run was 17 yards.

Jay Graham's second-quarter touchdown gave the Volunteers an added boost.

"We wanted to run rather than throw it, but Tennessee held up pretty well.

"They played great team defense."

The Vols got the Buckeyes completely out of their game plan.

Ohio State was so flustered that it wasn't even confident enough to try the middle of the line on its ill-fated option play in which Hoying bounced his option toss off the helmet of fullback Matt Calhoun. The pitch was intended for George.

It was simply a matter of the Vols guessing correctly, playing a six-man line and shooting Little in Hoying's face.

"We thought we should go outside, but they trumped us," Hoying said. "I thought the fullback was out of the way when I made the pitch, but I was wrong."

Little said the play was "a great call by (defensive coordinator) Coach (John) Chavis."

Both Ohio State coach John Cooper and offensive coordinator Joe Hollis defended the reasoning behind the option call, saying the Vols had stuffed the middle all afternoon.

"The option is a play that's worked before for us, but it didn't today," Hollis said.

"Tennessee had been overshifting to the unbalanced side, but they double-blitzed on that play."

The Vols needed the defense because the offense lacked much. Tennessee got two lengthy scoring plays, but no sustained drives.

Through the first three quarters, the Vols had snapped the ball just twice on Ohio State's side of the field.

"At halftime because of the rainy weather, we went back to doing simple things," Tennessee offensive coordinator David Cutcliffe said.

"We weren't try to score 50 points, we were just trying to win the game."

Vols' Defenders Stiffen vs. Tides' Last Gasp

By Ron Higgins
The Commercial Appeal

KNOXVILLE, Oct. 26, 1996

| Alabama | 0 | 3 | 10 | 0 | – | 13 |
| Tennessee | 0 | 0 | 6 | 14 | – | 20 |

Tennessee defensive end Leonard Little, breathing heavily after five straight Alabama pass plays, settled into his stance one last time today.

On the Vols' sideline, Tennessee quarterback Peyton Manning mouthed a silent prayer, "C'mon, Leonard."

With 39 seconds left to play, Leonard snuffed Alabama's final rally by raking the ball loose and decking Crimson Tide quarterback Freddie Kitchens on fourth and 10 at the Tennessee 11-yard line. The sack preserved the No. 6 Vols' 20-13 Southeastern Conference comeback victory over previously unbeaten No. 7 Alabama before 106,700 breathless fans at Neyland Stadium.

Volunteer defensive lineman Leonard Little wraps up Alabama halfback Dennis Riddle.

Dennis Riddle ran for a career-high 184 yards against Tennessee.

"I was so tired at the end I couldn't move," said Little, who lay motionless face down on the rain-slickened grass a couple of minutes after the play. "My legs had cramped. I was just waiting for the trainers to come get me."

Little's effort was typical of what the Volunteers needed to come back from a 13-0 deficit they stared at with 9:16 left in the third quarter. But with Tennessee relying on its defense to jumpstart a wheezing offense — a role change if there ever was one — Tennessee came back for the win that improved its record to 5-1 overall and 3-1 in the SEC.

After almost three quarters of getting kicked around by Alabama's defense, ranked fourth nationally, the Vols came to life with three touchdowns in the game's final 19:26. The game-winner was running back Jay Graham's 79-yard run with 2:17 left to play — a tough

Joey Kent scored on a 54-yard reception from Peyton Manning in the third quarter.

play to make on a day ruled by defenses.

"This was two evenly matched teams — it was a classic defensive battle," Tennessee coach Phillip Fulmer said. "We talked about it at halftime being a four-quarter game."

Alabama did just about everything it wanted to do. It held a 36:38-23:22 time of possession edge. It outgained the Vols, 327-296. It limited Manning to 176 yards — the first time this season he's thrown for less than 200 yards. It got a career-high 184 yards rushing from running back Dennis Riddle.

Yet the Crimson Tide walked away a loser to the Vols

for the second straight year because Kitchens was intercepted three times and Alabama couldn't produce points in the clutch.

"A game like this usually comes down to three or four plays — we didn't make those plays," said Alabama coach Gene Stallings, whose team fell to 7-1 overall and 4-1 in the SEC. "We played hard, but there were times when we needed to come away with points and didn't."

The Crimson Tide had 19 plays inside the Tennessee 20 and managed two Brian Cunningham field goals — the first a 36-yarder with 19 seconds left in the first half for a 3-0 halftime lead.

Tennessee made defensive stands in the second quarter and at game's end with the Tide knocking at the Vols' goal line. In between, Tennessee's offense finally jerked into gear after Alabama built a 13-0 lead with a 40-yard Kitchens to Marcell West TD pass and a 25-yard Cunningham field goal on the Tide's first two series of the second half.

But two plays swung momentum back towards the Vols.

The first was Manning's 54-yard touchdown pass to Joey Kent with 4:26 left in the third quarter. Alabama came with a seven-man rush, Manning switched plays — "I wanted to throw outside but Joey beat his man inside," Manning said — and he flipped a short pass over the middle to Kent who beat Alabama's Kevin Jackson.

Though Vols' placekicker Jeff Hall missed the extra point to leave Tennessee trailing, 13-6, the Vols kept coming even though Manning fumbled away a snap at the Alabama 22.

Kitchens had Alabama moving towards a clinching TD when the Vols produced big play No. 2. On third and 12 at the Tennessee 26, Tennessee's Terry Fair picked off Kitchens and scored on an 80-yard-plus return with 10:51 left to play.

The Vols were guilty of clipping, but Manning finally got time to throw three straight completions and Graham scored on a 5-yard run. Hall's PAT pulled Tennessee into a 13-13 tie with 9:41 left, and Alabama was clearly in trouble.

"We had them where we wanted them, and we just didn't finish the job," Kitchens said. "When you get Tennessee like that, you've got to finish 'em. We had plays called down there in scoring position that we could have connected on, but we didn't. We couldn't punch it in."

Jonathon Brown closes in on Dennis Riddle.

Alabama quarterback Freddie Kitchens gets leveled by a Vol lineman.

Vols Defense Snuffs Out Tide When It Counts

BY RON HIGGINS
The Commercial Appeal

KNOXVILLE

Tennessee cornerback Terry Fair and the rest of the Vols' defense were cognizant of the Southeastern Conference defensive rankings.

"We knew Alabama was No. 1 in the league and we were No. 2," Fair said after the game. "They probably still are No. 1, but maybe we moved up in the eyes of some people."

Maybe Fair was referring to the Tide's offense as the new admirers. The Vols intercepted erratic Alabama quarterback Freddie Kitchens three times, twice by Fair himself, and stopped the Tide four downs at the Alabama 11 in the final minute to boost Tennessee to a 20-13 win at Neyland Stadium.

In an old-time defensive battle that earmarked many of the games in the 1960's, 70's and 80's between these teams, the Vols came up huge time after time when the Tide's offense was pressing for points.

True, Alabama gained 327 yards and running back Dennis Riddle ran for 184 yards on 38 carries — both career highs. But when it came time to keep the Tide out of the end zone, the Vols stepped up.

"Although the Ohio State game (last year's win over the Buckeyes in the Citrus Bowl) ranks right up there, this defensive performance is the best I've seen since I've been here," Tennessee coach Phillip Fulmer said. "Our defense gave us a phenomenal effort and put us in a position to win. They were challenged by themselves and the coaching staff all week."

Fair gave up a touchdown when he miscommunicated a coverage and watched Kitchens throw a 40-yard TD pass to a wide-open Marcell West for a 10-0 lead with 11:42 left in the third quarter.

But he atoned with an interception that set the table for the Vols' game-tying TD. He returned Kitchens' pass 80-plus yards for a score, but a clipping call set the ball back at the Alabama 43 with 10:51 left in the fourth quarter.

"He (West) tried a curl route and I just anticipated him running that route," Fair said. "I stepped in front and picked it off. I didn't know it was called back (because of the clipping) until I got to the sidelines. I was just glad I put us in position to

Dennis Riddle rips through an opening in the Volunteer defense.

score and we took advantage."

The Vols' defense had its problems at times dealing with Kitchens, who was 8-for-23 for 137 yards. He was so uneven — one minute he was throwing a TD pass to West and the next minute he was being intercepted or flinging bad passes — that the Vols defense didn't know what to make of him.

"He's one tough guy — he weighs about 235 and it's like having a linebacker back there playing quarterback," Tennessee defensive end Leonard Little said. "But on that last series, you could see he was getting timid. We were getting a good rush and our backs

were covering their receivers."

On that game-saving goal-line stand, one Kitchens pass was tipped away, two were overthrown on corner routes and Little blasted the ball loose from Kitchens on fourth down.

"They were just about out of plays to run," said Tennessee strong safety Tori Noel of Memphis' Melrose High. "They kept running the same pass route. We knew what they were doing."

Peyton Manning passed for 408 yards and four touchdowns, and ran for another TD.

" That was our best offensive game, this year, by far. The way we started things off with a bang (jumping to a 21-0 first-quarter lead) reminded me of the way we played last year. "

TENNESSEE QUARTERBACK PEYTON MANNING

Manning Shreds 'Cats, 48-28, in Citrus Bowl

BY RON HIGGINS
The Commercial Appeal

ORLANDO, Jan. 1, 1997

Northwestern	0	21	0	7	–	28
Tennessee	21	10	7	10	–	48

Tennessee junior quarterback Peyton Manning, helmet in hand, grinned broadly and shook his head.

The final seconds of the Vols' 48-28 Citrus Bowl victory over Northwestern were ticking away today, and Manning's teammates were leading the Big Orange faithful in the crowd of 63,467 in making one last plea for Manning to bypass entering the NFL draft and return for his senior season.

The more the crowd chanted "One More Year, One More Year" and "Stay Peyton Stay," the more he smiled. If indeed Manning's Vols' career is over, it was a memorable way to end it.

Manning, voted the bowl's Most Valuable Player, looked like a pro, standing tall behind superb protection and zipping penetrating throws for 408 yards and four touchdowns through the step-too-slow defense of the Big 10 co-champion Wildcats. It was the second-most passing yards in the bowl's 51-year history. He also scored on an impromptu 10-yard naked bootleg in which he read the defense and decided to keep the ball instead of handing off.

"That was the most fun we've had in a while," said Manning, who said he won't be rushed into making a decision about his future. "That was our best offensive game, this year, by far. The way we started things off with a bang (jumping to a 21-0 first-quarter lead) reminded me of the way we played last year. Even our offensive line was excited, and I'd hadn't seen that much this year."

The win helped Tennessee finish 10-2, the third time in four seasons under Coach Phillip Fulmer that the Vols have won 10 or more games. It also assured a second straight Associated Press Top 10 finish for currently No. 9 Tennessee, something it last did in 1989 and 1990.

"It's a great accomplishment to have back-to-back 10-win seasons," said Fulmer, whose team last year finished 11-1 with a 20-14 Citrus Bowl victory over Ohio State. "We talked about setting the tempo in the first five minutes of each half of this game and we did that."

Except for a 5:28 span in the second quarter when Northwestern scored three times to pull into a 21-21 tie against the self-destructing, penalty-prone Vols, Tennessee used its superior speed to dazzle the Wildcats offensively and defensively.

While Manning was leading an offense that rolled for 523 yards and averaged 7.4 yards per play — by halftime the Vols had scored more points and gained more yardage than Northwestern had previously been allowing per game — the Vols' defense fared rather well.

Again thriving on the challenge of playing sup-

> *" It's a great accomplishment to have back-to-back 10-win seasons. We talked about setting the tempo in the first five minutes of each half of this game and we did that. "*
>
> TENNESSEE COACH PHILLIP FULMER

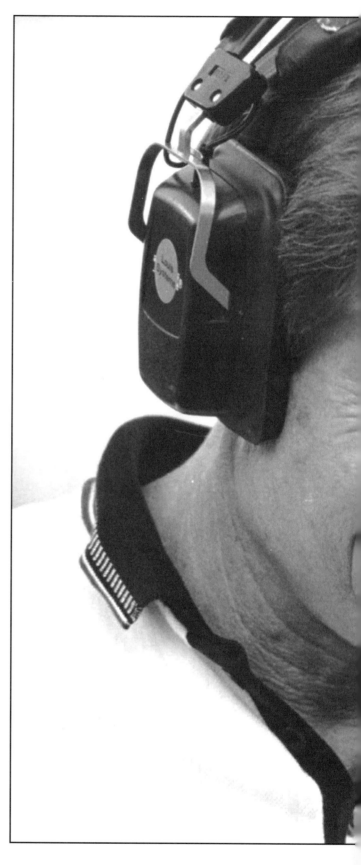

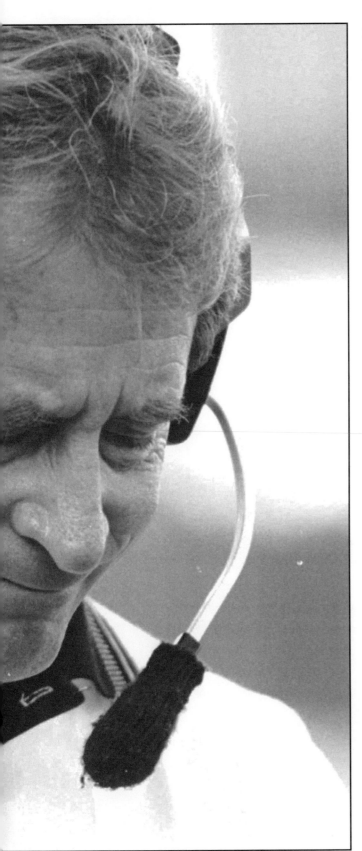

posedly a more physical Big 10 team led by a bruising all-league tailback, Tennessee held Northwestern to 285 yards. Tailback Darnell Autry, slowed by the flu and the Vols, scored twice but gained just 66 yards.

Northwestern coach Gary Barnett, whose team finished 9-3, knew before the game the Vols' speed would be a problem. And it was.

"We couldn't block their speed," Barnett said.

The Vols scored on their first three possessions with Manning's TD run sandwiched by his scoring strikes of 43 yards to Peerless Price and 10 yards to Joey Kent.

Northwestern took an opening the Vols gave them in the second quarter. Following a 13-yard punt by Northwestern's Paul Burton to the Northwestern 37, Tennessee wasted an offensive series by getting too cute. It ran two trick plays, neither one worked, the Vols punted and the Wildcats used 42 yards of Tennessee defensive penalties to drive 80 yards for a confidence-building 2-yard TD by Autry.

The Wildcats, this year's college football king of comebacks, rang up a 20-yard Steve Schnur to Brian Musso TD pass and a 28-yard Autry scoring run after a fumble by the Vols' Jay Graham. And in a blink, it was 21-21 with 2:27 left before the half.

> " *We couldn't block their speed.* "
>
> NORTHWESTERN
> COACH GARY
> BARNETT

That was enough time for 10 Tennessee points — Manning's 67-yard TD throw to Kent followed by an 81-yard drive in the final 1:11 that led to Jeff Hall's 19-yard field goal for a 31-21 lead as the horn sounded to end the first half.

Tennessee linebacker Tyrone Hines snuffed any more thoughts about a Northwestern comeback. He intercepted a Schnur pass on the third play of the second half and rambled 30 yards for a touchdown for a 38-21 lead.

Frustrated Northwestern coach Gary Barnett on the sidelines after the game.

Tennessee Rips 'Bama, Keeps SEC Title Hopes Alive

BY DAVID WILLIAMS
The Commercial Appeal

BIRMINGHAM, Oct. 18, 1997

There were curtain calls and victory cigars. There was quarterback Peyton Manning, after leading the University of Tennessee football team to a 38-21 victory over rival Alabama, leading the UT band as well.

What, you wonder, might the celebration at Legion Field have looked like if the day had been perfect?

Perfection was denied the Volunteers before they took the field tonight, but it didn't show. Perfection would have been a Florida loss to Auburn earlier in the day, because it would have put the Vols in control of the Southeastern Conference Eastern Division race.

But before 83,091 witnesses, the Vols stuffed Alabama, and also the speculation that a Gator victory might leave them emotionally flat for their own game.

Tennessee's Marcus Nash rips past a fallen Alabama defensive back.

Tennessee	7	14	10	7	–	38
Alabama	6	0	8	7	–	21

Volunteer defensive lineman Shawn Ellis locks up on Alabama quarterback Freddie Kitchens.

"We kept saying and meant it — from the very beginning of the week — it did not matter," UT coach Phillip Fulmer said of the Florida game. "It was either going to be a great win or a greater win. If we got a win, it was a great day."

How great?

■ Manning passed for 304 yards and three touchdowns, and had his first interception-free game of the season.

■ The Tennessee defense held Alabama to 225 yards total offense, including 6 yards rushing in the first half.

■ The Volunteers won their third straight game in a series dominated in recent years by Alabama.

■ The Vols (5-1 overall, 3-1 in the SEC) may not have taken overtaken Florida, but they stayed on course for a major bowl, and remain poised to strike if Florida stumbles before season's end.

"More than likely, a lot of people looked down on us because we lost to Florida, and were sort of down," wide receiver Jeremaine Copeland said of the Vols' 33-20 loss to the Gators on Sept. 20. "But we're not. We're a team that's coming back together.

Alabama coach Mike DuBose congratulates Vols coach Phil Fulmer after the game.

"I think this is the big victory that Tennessee needed to keep us on that victory roll from here to the end of the season."

Copeland, who had six catches for 70 yards and two touchdowns, claimed he didn't even know the Florida-Auburn outcome. "I guess Florida won, maybe," he said, smiling.

Other players said they heard the final score — Florida 24, Auburn 10 — over the Legion Field public address system.

"It went in one ear and out the other," said linebacker Leonard Little.

You might have wondered otherwise in the first few minutes, though.

Manning was sacked on UT's first play and the Vols were quickly punting. Alabama took the ball and drove it down the field, inside the Tennessee 25 before stalling and settling for a 42-yard Brian Cunningham field goal and 3-0 lead.

Tennessee punted on its second possession, then true freshman running back Jamal Lewis fumbled on

the third. The Alabama offense, handed the ball on the UT 20, again settled for a Cunningham field goal, this a 35-yarder.

"It was tough early on," Manning said. "We had the sack on the first play. We turned it over. Fortunately our defense came through."

It was late first quarter now, and the Vols awoke with a vengeance — and a message: It'll take more than field goals to beat this team.

The Vols put together three straight touchdown drives — 74 yards on nine plays, 80 yards on 11 plays and 63 yards on five plays — to make a game of it, then a rout of it. The offensive explosion didn't take much more than five minutes.

A fourth would-be scoring drive failed when a 29-yard Jeff Hall field goal was blocked.

"Once we got on track, things became a little bit easier," Manning said.

By halftime, then, it was 21-6 and everything right with Tennessee and wrong with Alabama this season had been on display.

Another High Note for Manning

By Geoff Calkins
The Commercial Appeal

BIRMINGHAM

OK, I've seen enough.
Fly him to New York.
Put him in a new suit.
Hand him the Heisman.

Peyton Manning had a nice little night against Alabama. He threw three touchdown passes. He beat Alabama for the third time in three years, 38-21. Then he celebrated by climbing a ladder in the end zone and conducting the Tennessee marching band in a joyous, brassy, but slightly disjointed rendition of *Rocky Top*.

Manning's assessment of his orchestral debut?

"There was a guy in the back who was off key," he said. "That was my fault."

There is a sneering contingent that thinks Manning will win the Heisman as a sort of lifetime achievement award. That would be just fine if it were true. Manning is a good guy. He has had a wonderful career. He brought honor to college football by announcing in March that he planned to stay around for his senior year.

But those who say Manning will win the Heisman because of what he said this spring should have seen what he did tonight.

Granted, this isn't a good Alabama team. Truth be told, this wouldn't be a good North Alabama team. The biggest cheer of the night might have come when the public address guy announced that Notre Dame

Peyton Manning passed for 304 yards and three touchdowns against Alabama.

had lost again. Misery had company.

But Tennessee didn't exactly come out all cranked up and ready to go, either. Tennessee's players learned just before the game that Florida had defeated Auburn, essentially ending any hope that Tennessee might make it to the SEC Championship. As pep talks go, this wasn't Rockne material.

Tennessee came out flat. Freshman whiz Jamal Lewis fumbled deep in Tennessee territory. Alabama built a 6-0 lead on defense, luck and emotion.

"We were struggling at the beginning," said head coach Phil Fulmer. "We knew we were in a game."

Which is about when Manning started firing away, started stringing together completions, started updating his Heisman resume.

Manning never looks as smooth as some national observers expect. He's gangly. He's awkward. He's all smarts and accuracy and timing. If he were a baseball pitcher, he'd be a changeup guy like Greg Maddux, not a fastball guy like Roger Clemens.

Trailing six-zip, Manning started throwing strikes. He didn't do anything spectacular. He didn't throw that perfect pass that everyone will remember. He completed five passes to four different receivers to move his team inside the Alabama 20.

Then, with Alabama expecting the pass, Manning slipped the ball to Shawn Bryson on a draw. Tennessee led. Bryson had never scored an easier touchdown.

"That was the one we needed," said Manning. "It got it rolling."

Manning kept firing away. He finished with more than 300 yards (304) for the seventh straight time. That's not the work of a guy who will win the Heisman on reputation.

And then Manning conducted the band. Hey, it made sense at the time. It was his last game against Alabama. It was his last trip to Birmingham.

"It was something I always wanted to do," said Manning, said the man who is favored to win the Heisman. "It's great to go out on a high note."

Vols Rally to Defeat Auburn in SEC Title Thriller

By David Williams
The Commercial Appeal

Atlanta, Dec. 6, 1997

The No. 3 University of Tennessee Volunteers won the Southeastern Conference football championship, then had to wonder:

Was a rousing-but-ragged, come-from-behind 30-29 victory over No. 11 Auburn impressive enough for the Vols to hold their ranking and remain in the national championship race?

If the Vols hold firm in the polls, the victory likely puts them in the Jan. 2 Orange Bowl against No. 2 Nebraska, which beat Texas A&M today for the Big 12 title.

If top-ranked Michigan loses the Jan. 1 Rose Bowl to Washington State, the Orange Bowl could decide the national title.

Freshman Jamal Lewis (31) dives high against the Auburn defense.

| Tennessee | 7 | 3 | 13 | 7 | – | 30 |
| Auburn | 13 | 7 | 9 | 0 | – | 29 |

No matter their bowl fate, the Vols (11-1) are in the Alliance Bowl selection group and are SEC conference champions.

"We had to get going and make enough plays to win the game," said UT quarterback Peyton Manning. "We worked so hard to get here and win the SEC ... That's all that matters."

Tonight, before 76,896 in the Georgia Dome, they overcame their own mistakes and an Auburn team that struggled with its own inefficiencies. Manning had two interceptions, but passed for four touchdowns to lift the Eastern Division winners. He finished the game with 25 completions on 43 attempts for 373 yards.

"We just didn't make enough big plays to win the game," said Auburn coach Terry Bowden.

Game Statistics

	UT	AU
First downs	22	9
Rushes-Yards	36-129	21-(-15)
Passing	373	262
Return yards	188	205
Comp-Att-Int	25-43-2	14-34-0
Punts	5-36.4	10-43.8
Fumbles-Lost	6-4	5-1
Penalties-Yards	9-49	12-78
Time of possession	35:43	24:17

Tennessee opened the game with a swift and staggering blow to Auburn (9-3), the SEC Western Division champs. Then the Vols proceeded to play perhaps their worst half of the season.

First for the good part for UT: Manning led a five-play, 80-yard scoring drive capped with a perfect 40-yard pass to Peerless Price for the touchdown. Just over two minutes had elapsed and the SEC's top-rated offense had struck.

Auburn took the blow, shrugged and answered with a scoring drive of its own, ending with a 30-yard Jaret Holmes field goal. The big play came when the UT defense forced Auburn quarterback Dameyune Craig to scramble — making him more dangerous — and he connected with Hicks Poor for a 69-yard gain.

From there, the half was a story of Tennessee giveaways — five fumbles, three of them recovered by Auburn, and an interception by Manning.

Two of the fumbles were by wide receiver Marcus Nash, and one of those was returned 24 yards by free safety Brad Ware for a touchdown and a 10-7 Auburn lead.

The other part of the first-half story, though, was

Auburn's inability to completely take charge of the game. They led, 20-10, at the half — a game still very much in reach for UT. With Craig as their lone weapon, they were unable to turn turnovers into touchdowns.

Auburn's offense scored only one first half touchdown — a beautiful 51-yard pass from Craig to Tyrone Goodson, who was draped by Vols cornerback Terry Fair. Fair later fumbled back-to-back punt returns — the first at the end of a splendid 44-yard return that set an SEC championship-game record.

The second half arrived, and so did the Vols, looking very much like the No. 3 team in the nation. The defense quickly forced Auburn to punt and Fair returned it 45 yards to the Auburn 22. Manning took it from there, leading a quick touchdown drive ending with a 5-yard pass to Jermaine Copeland.

Down, 20-17, now and feeding on the momentum shift, the Vols' defense again stuffed Auburn and its one-dimensional offense. The Vols' offense soon was on the move again, inside Auburn territory, inside the 20, then Manning threw a pass that went in and out of Copeland's hands and to Auburn cornerback Jason Bray.

From the Auburn 4, Bray returned it 77 yards, setting up the Auburn offense for an easy touchdown. This time, the Tigers converted, with Craig lofting a 24-yard scoring pass to fullback Fred Beasley for a 27-17 lead.

The Vols answered with a touchdown drive, with Manning throwing a 46-yard scoring pass to Price. The extra point by Jeff Hall would cut the lead to 3, but — in another strange twist — the kick was blocked and returned the length of the field by Auburn's Quinton Reese for 2 points. The Tigers now led, 29-23.

And back Tennessee's offense came, again driving into Auburn territory — and again giving up the ball, this time as Manning was handing off to Lewis. It was the Vols' sixth turnover. The Tigers couldn't move the ball, but a little more time had passed and another UT offensive threat had passed.

But you knew the Vols weren't finished. On their next possession, Manning passed to Nash, who broke free of the defense and sprinted for the TD — a 73-yard play — and, with Hall's extra point, a 30-29 lead with 11:14 left in the game.

It was a slim lead, but it was enough.

Peerless Price scored two touchdowns on 40-yard and 46-yard receptions.

Volunteers Weren't Pretty, But Had the Stuff to Win

By Geoff Calkins
The Commercial Appeal

Peyton Manning leapt in celebration. Leonard Little flung himself into the stands. Spencer Riley hoisted an enormous Tennessee flag and started off on an impromptu victory lap around the stadium.

Happy ending?

Happy ending.

Suddenly, this enormous, sprawling, complicated mess of a football season seemed to make all the sense in the world.

The Tennessee Volunteers defeated the Auburn Tigers tonight, 30-29. The Vols won their first SEC championship since 1990. The Vols also won a game that could be the final piece — well, not the final piece, that could be saved for later, for Miami — in a season that seems to fit just fine.

The men in orange could be bound for the bowl of the same color. Never mind the year that preceded it. Never mind the aesthetic quality of the game that produced it. If that's the way things worked out — and we'll find out tomorrow afternoon, when the bowl bids are announced — how much more symmetrical can things get?

"It's just was Tennessee's year," said Auburn coach Terry Bowden. "They've been the bridesmaid, but no more."

Oh, this game was a mess. A hideous, jumbled wreck of a game. You got the feeling Nebraska might have been snickering. You got the feeling SEC commissioner Roy Kramer might have been cringing. You got the feeling the Orange Bowl just might contem-

plate taking Florida State instead of Tennessee.

Besides all that, you got the feeling that the Vols might have misunderstood their coach's pregame exhortation. Prior to kickoff, UT head coach Phil Fulmer let the media in on his plan: "We're going to shoot all our bullets and see what happens."

Yeah, well. Who knew the Vols would be firing most of them into their feet?

It was impossible to keep up with the bumbles, impossible to even count them, much less keep track:

■ The Vols turned the ball over six times.

■ Terry Fair turned the ball over twice within two minutes.

■ Marcus Nash fumbled twice and dropped a handful of passes.

■ Auburn blocked a Tennessee extra point and returned it for two points of its own.

With all that having happened, the Vols still persevered and won.

If there is any hallmark of this football team, that may be it. Other Tennessee teams have been prettier. Other Tennessee teams have been more elegant. But few have been more adept at fighting through difficult circumstances.

That's what happened in this one, in the end. Tennessee kept firing. Tennessee kept working. Tennessee finally connected.

With 11 minutes and change remaining in the game, Manning took a quick drop and fired a hard out to Nash. And Nash — he of the previous drops, he of the previous fumbles — broke a handful of tackles and scampered 73 yards for the game-winning touchdown.

And that was it, that was the difference. It was all over but the shouting.

And though the bowl bid is still up in the air, the SEC championship belongs to Tennessee, at last.

Jamal Lewis (31) attracted a crowd of Auburn defenders, who wanted to strip him of the football late in the game.

Manning Is Game's MVP

Peyton Manning finished the game with 25 completions for 373 yards and four touchdowns.

Peyton Manning holds every game, season and career passing record in Tennessee Vols football history, and he owns his share of SEC records as well. It didn't take Manning long tonight to add to his record collection and win the game's Most Valuable Player honors along the way.

On Tennessee's first snap, he completed a 25-yard swing pass to tailback Jamal Lewis. That completion was No. 839 in his career, breaking a tie with former Georgia quarterback Eric Zeier atop the SEC list.

On Tennessee's first drive, Manning completed 3 of 3 passes for 72 yards, including a 40-yard touchdown pass. Those 72 yards pushed Manning past last year's

Heisman winner, Danny Wuerffel, into second place on the SEC career chart for passing yards.

Manning needed 226 yards passing overall today to surpass Zeier as the SEC career leader. Manning finished with 25 completions on 43 attempts for 373 yards and four touchdowns to shatter Zeier's SEC career records for completions, passing yardage and total offense.

After leading the Vols from behind for their first SEC title since 1990, Manning told the assembled media after the game: "This is why you play in the SEC."

His coach, Phil Fulmer, added: "This is why you stay for your fourth year."

Peyton Manning: More Than a Hero

BY DAVID WILLIAMS
The Commercial Appeal

Where to begin?
Wherever it is, it's not with the numbers. How do you put an odometer on a folk hero?

Which is what he was, is and ever shall be in the land of blue tick coon hounds and orange-and-white checkerboard end zones.

Peyton Manning, folk hero.

No mere football legend, this one. No simple passing fancy. Someday, the University of Tennessee will build a statue of him and have to decide whether to even have him in a football stance.

To pick the pose of Peyton Manning, standing straight and tall in the pocket with a blitz all about him, is to miss the one of him joyously leading the Pride of the Southland band through *Rocky Top* after leading the Volunteers past Alabama for the third straight year.

Or the one of him in cap and gown, having graduated in three years with a 3.6 grade-point-average that was first among all UT speech communications majors.

Or the one of him telling the world that the National Football League and its millions could wait, that "I've made up my mind and I don't expect to look back ... I'm staying at the University of Tennessee."

Or — well, you get the picture.

Rather, you get dozens of them. Hundreds. Which is maybe how many statues they'll need to capture the essence of Peyton Williams Manning, folk hero.

HIS FIRST APPEARANCE in a college football game was nothing much to talk about, and so naturally it's a story Manning loves to tell.

It was Sept. 3, 1994. Tennessee had traveled to Pasadena, Calif., to play UCLA. Manning was an 18-year-old freshman, a prize recruit biding his time while Jerry Colquitt, a fifth-year senior, quar-

YOUNG STUDENT: Former NFL quarterback Archie Manning calls the signals for young Peyton. "He was studying me," his father once said.

16 RETIRED: In his final season, Manning passed for 3,819 yards and 36 TDs — both career highs — and became the SEC's career passing leader with 11,201 yards.

terbacked the Vols.

Then, on the seventh play of the game, Colquitt's season ended with a knee injury.

Manning was one of three reserve quarterbacks UT called on that day, and when he arrived in the huddle he was eager to be everything that he would, in time, become.

"I got in the huddle," he would say, "and told the guys, 'I know I'm just a freshman, but I can take us down the field.'"

It was inspiring stuff, very rah-rah. But there being a time and a place for everything, and this being neither the time nor the place, a veteran linemen said to Manning:

"Shut up and call the play."

Said the rookie to the veteran: "Yes, sir."

When they have all the Manning statues built and get around to making a movie of him, that scene will have to be in it. It says more about Manning than all of his 11,201 career passing yards and his 89 touchdown passes.

It tells you that for all his maturity — which is

so evident in his public speaking, his media interviews, his school work — there was a lot of little boy in him. He will ride a lot of limos in his day, but it's far easier to imagine him wheeling up to the stadium on a mud-caked bike with banana seat and Johnny Unitas cards in the spokes, and saying, "Let's play."

He loved the game, he prized it. One senses that from that first day in Pasadena, Manning never entered the UT huddle without at least wanting to say, "I can take us down the field."

And he could, and he would, and he did.

Dozens of times. Hundreds. And sooner that anyone imagined.

Four games into that 1994 season, another Tennessee quarterback, Todd Helton, was lost to injury.

The timetable was to be scrapped, the future had suddenly arrived. And it was wearing No. 16 and an aw-shucks grin.

Manning went on to start eight games that freshman year, winning seven. He completed 18 of 23 pass-

es for 189 yards and three touchdowns against South Carolina — shades of the machine-like efficiency to come. He completed nearly 62 percent of his passes for the season, and was named Southeastern Conference freshman of the year.

He had come a long way in a short time, a long way from that day in Pasadena when he shut up, handed off the ball three times, then retreated to the sidelines for the day.

By his sophomore year, he was a national sensation as the Vols finished 11-1, losing only to their nemesis, and Manning's — Florida. The year ended with a 20-14 defeat of Ohio State in the Citrus Bowl and a No. 3 ranking.

Manning was first-team all-SEC, a finalist for the Davey O'Brien Quarterback Award, sixth in the Heisman Trophy voting.

More than all of that, he had arrived. He had become a veteran, a leader.

"Peyton gives you that peace of mind that he knows what to do each and every play," wide receiver Joey Kent said.

It was, in some ways, Manning's best season. Consider: He completed 244 of 380 passes — 64.2 percent — for 22 touchdowns and four interceptions. His percentage of passes intercepted — 1.1 — is in the NCAA record book.

SO PEYTON MANNING WAS SPECTACULARLY GIFTED. That
is a given. He had the size, the arm strength, the quick release. He didn't just read defenses — he broke their codes.

But does that explain why he would have a giraffe named after him?

That happened in 1996 at the Knoxville Zoo, where executive director Patrick M.M. Roddy explained, "We respect Peyton a great deal and want him to know we're all cheering for him ..."

It was an easy thing to do, cheering for Manning, because as much as he was an up-to-the-minute version of the strong, strapping late-20th century college quarterback, Manning seemed more like the heroes of old. He seemed larger than life but, in his eyes, no better than anyone else.

Maybe, for that reason, people not only idolized him but also identified with him.

Which still may not explain why someone would name a giraffe after him, but it will have to do. What seems clear, though, is this: So many of the great players today can't live outside their jerseys. They need the field under their feet, or they can't stand up for falling down.

They are poor students, or poor citizens — poor examples to all the young, would-be football players who might seek to follow them.

But you could take Manning anywhere. You could take him to an elementary school and have him talk of putting education above sports, with no hint of hypocrisy in the air.

You could follow him anywhere — to class, to the stadium, to any number of public appearances — and never expect to be led astray.

AS QUARTERBACKS GO, he was the son of a gun.

His daddy was Archie Manning, himself a quarterback legend. All-American at Ole Miss. All-pro with

the NFL's New Orleans Saints. Peyton grew up around the game. It was child's play for him. That, and a life's calling.

So, of course, he grew up to become a great quarterback. He had the quarterback gene. It was fate.

There was a temptation to say so, at least. Say it, and Peyton Manning would gently — or maybe not so gently — tell you otherwise. He worked too hard, studied too long, to believe such bunk.

"So many of you out there now are probably wondering, 'What makes Peyton Manning tick?'" he told one audience. "What route did I take to achieve my goals? Well, I can assure you this: It's not the glory that's driven me to excel over the years. And it's not my parents.

"It's something inside me."

YOU COULDN'T MISS PEYTON MANNING on the football field — 6-foot-5 and 222 pounds with the air of a leader from white helmet to black high-topped shoes — but you had to watch closely his junior year.

Because you thought it might be his last.

By the modern-day nature of things, 1996 should have been Manning's final college season, and what a way to go out: He became the first Tennessee quarterback to pass for more than 3,000 yards in a season and led the Vols to a 10-2 record.

The last day of the 1996 season he was spectacular, passing for 408 yards, two touchdowns and no interceptions as UT whipped Northwestern, 48-28, in the Citrus Bowl. It was, at the end, a game of chants.

"One more year, one more year," the Tennessee fans shouted to Manning.

Manning, meanwhile, was reveling in that day, that game, not the business of playing for pay.

"That was the most fun we've had in a while," he said. "That was our best offensive game this year, by far. The way we started things off with a bang (21-0 in the first quarter) reminded me of the way we played last year (in 1995). Even our offensive line was excited, and I hadn't seen that much (excitement) this year."

Long after the fact, you can pick that quote apart for clues. They're all there. It was as plain as the T on his helmet. Here was a player who played for fun, for the excitement in the eyes of his teammates.

As for Peyton Manning's eyes, you didn't look into them and see dollar signs.

You saw a searching for more — one more year of fun, one more year of challenges, one more year for another crack at Florida, another run at a championship.

One more year, period.

Still, two months passed before Manning ended the speculation in a press conference at UT's Thompson-Boling Arena. His parents, Archie and Olivia, were there. So was a room-full of media and a national TV audience. Well, Peyton?

Then he said what college athletes so rarely say these days — that the college experience is priceless.

"Tennessee people through the generations have held loyalty and commitment in the very highest regard," said head coach Phillip Fulmer. "Today, we are blessed with the ultimate return of loyalty and commitment."

But it was no mere victory lap around the nation's college campuses.

Manning still had much to do, much to achieve. He hadn't won the Heisman Trophy. He hadn't led the Volunteers past Florida. He hadn't led them to a championship.

In the season to come, he realized only one of those goals — Tennessee won the SEC East and beat Auburn in the league championship game — but it was nonetheless a glorious year.

It was, beyond that, pure Peyton Manning.

Consider the way he lost the Heisman Trophy — with a grace many players lack in winning it.

During the season, he couldn't escape the Heisman questions. They were there after every game. But the strain didn't show. Put the weight of the world on Peyton Manning's shoulders, and still he could shrug them.

"You can't go out and try to win an individual award like the Heisman Trophy," he said. "When you do that, you hurt yourself. You're making bad decisions and you're hurting your team."

And so he set about winning games. He passed for 3,819 yards and 36 touchdowns — both career highs — and along the way became the SEC's career passing leader with 11,201 yards.

But he didn't win them all.

Florida beat Tennessee, again, in 1997. Manning had a big day statistically, but had an interception returned 89 yards for a touchdown. Tennessee was driving at the time, and a touchdown would have tied it. Instead, it was 14-0, Gators.

When it was over, the season was only three games old, and it seemed lost. The Eastern Division — a championship — seemed out of reach. So did a national championship.

Oh, well, there was always the Heisman.

Manning and his fellow Volunteer seniors didn't buy all that talk about the season being lost, of course. The team kept winning and waiting to see if Florida would stumble. The Gators did, losing twice to give UT the division title and a place in the SEC championship game in a sold-out Georgia Dome, where Manning passed for 373 yards and four touchdowns.

A few days later, Manning lost the Heisman — inexplicably to many — to Michigan defensive back Charles Woodson, an underdog candidate who seemed to benefit from a sort of Manning backlash.

A MAN IN DEMAND: Peyton was the first pick in the 1998 NFL Draft by the Indianapolis Colts.

Manning had been so widely presumed to be the Heisman frontrunner, from that day he announced he would return for his senior season, there seemed almost a movement among voters to champion someone else, anyone else.

Still, in defeat, Manning was Manning.

"I'd be less than honest if I didn't say that I wanted this award because of the people back home in Tennessee," he said. "In a lot of ways, I wanted to win it for them. So I apologize to them because they've been so supportive of me."

That was Peyton for you — apologizing to Vol fans.

It's why they loved him, why they'll never forget him.

One more time, it was how he became what he is, was and ever shall be in the land of blue tick coon hounds and orange-and-white checkerboard end zones.

Peyton Manning, folk hero.

With Gators closing in, Vols quarterback Tee Martin (17) looks for a receiver in the end zone.

At Long Last, Vols End Futility vs. Gators

BY DAVID WILLIAMS
The Commercial Appeal

Knoxville, Sept. 19, 1998

| Florida | 3 | 7 | 7 | 0 | 0 | – | 17 |
| Tennessee | 7 | 3 | 7 | 0 | 3 | – | 20 |

The streak is dead. The Neyland Stadium goalposts aren't in such great shape, either.

Tennessee's Jeff Hall kicked a 41-yard field goal in overtime to lift the No. 6 Volunteers to a 20-17 victory tonight over No. 2 Florida, ending the Gators' five-year dominance in the Southeastern Conference Eastern Division powers' rivalry.

Florida's Collins Cooper could have tied it, but his 32-yarder was wide to the left. Then thousands of orange-clad fans from the stadium-record crowd of 107,653 flooded onto the field, ripping out the fateful goalpost in mere seconds.

"It was a great battle right to the end, and past the end," said Tennessee coach Phillip Fulmer, who is now 2-5 against Florida.

Hall also kicked the game-winning field goal in the Vols' season-opening 34-33 victory over Syracuse. This victory, though, had all sorts of heroes.

Linebacker Al Wilson forced three fumbles in the first half, setting a school single-game record. On offense, Jamal Lewis overcame a slow start to finish with 82 yards rushing. Also, Shawn Bryson had a 57-yard touchdown run. And quarterback Tee Martin, despite only completing 7-of-20 for 64 yards and an interception, kept mistakes to a minimum and had a touchdown pass.

Florida, meanwhile, earned the loss the old-fashioned way — losing four fumbles and also throwing an interception.

The overtime finish was fitting, because the game was tight throughout.

Tennessee got the ball first in the overtime, starting at the Florida 25. The Vols immediately went for a touchdown, but Martin missed two end zone passes. A holding penalty then backed the Vols into the far reaches of field goal range, but Martin's 14-yard scramble brought them back in.

Then Hall nailed his field goal.

Florida, which all night alternated quarterbacks Jesse Palmer and Doug Johnson on nearly every play, had a more promising start to its possession. The Gators drove to the Vols' 15 for a first down, but neither Palmer nor Johnson could take them farther.

Then came Cooper for his 32-yard try. He missed it, and the place went crazy.

"Our fans are absolutely incredible," Fulmer said. "That's the first thing I told our team, to count our blessings that we have a chance to play at a great school with a great tradition like Tennessee has.

"They were there in force and certainly a factor in the ballgame. (They were) as loud as anybody's (fans) in America."

The previous five years, the game seemed to be won when it was only getting started. In four of the five Florida victories during the streak, the Gators led by at least two touchdowns early in the second quarter.

Last year, with UT trailing, 7-0, but driving late in the first quarter, Peyton Manning unloaded a pass under heavy pressure and was intercepted by Tony George, whose 89-yard return for a touchdown gave Florida a 14-0 lead.

The Gators had leads of 24-0 in 1994 and 35-0 in 1996. The one year the Volunteers struck quickly, the Gators struck back, turning a 30-14 deficit into a 62-37 victory in 1995. This time, defenses dominated and neither team could pull away.

Palmer completed 16-of-23 passes for 210 yards, an interception and two touchdowns. Johnson completed 15-of-26 for 199 yards. That added up to a big passing day, but only 17 points.

Tennessee held the Gators to minus-13 yards rushing.

The Gators started well, driving to the Tennessee 3-yard-line on their first possession, but tailback Terry Jackson fumbled into the end zone. Wilson caused it, Raynoch Thompson recovered, and UT had dodged early trouble.

More than 40,000 Volunteer fans mobbed the field after the game, tearing down both goalposts.

"Obviously turnovers were the difference," Fulmer said. It was the Volunteers' first overtime game, and was seen by the largest crowd in stadium history. The record had been the 107,608 who packed in for the Florida game in 1996.

That crowd left dejected. This one floated home.

Ball Sails Left
And the Earth Moves

By Geoff Calkins
The Commercial Appeal

The press box is shaking.

Actually shaking.

Physically shaking.

Somewhere-a-Richter-scale-should-be-recording-this-shaking.

So this is what joy feels like at Neyland Stadium. So this is what it feels like to beat Florida. It had been so long, it had been so long, some off us never knew.

Did you see it? Did you see this incredible game?

And can you see the way it ended, still?

Florida kicker Collins Cooper lined up at the right hash mark. In overtime. Just 32 yards away from a field goal that would have tied the game.

Cooper took his steps. Swung his foot into the ball. Watched as it skittered wide left. And then it was bedlam, utter bedlam.

It took maybe five seconds for the first goalpost to come down. It took maybe five more seconds for the next one to come down. It may take a good deal longer for the shaking to stop.

"We did it," someone is yelling.

"We did it, we did it, we did it!"

They did do it. And they did it in a way Tennessee fans will remember for a very long time.

The team that everyone said couldn't beat Florida — the team that had lost to the Gators five times in a row — ended that streak with a perfectly thrilling, perfectly exhausting, 20-17 overtime win.

"I don't know who played well and who didn't," said head coach Phillip Fulmer.

"But I'm glad to come out on top."

Where to start? Where to begin? Tennessee had heroes all over the field.

There was Shawn Bryson, the fullback, bursting 57 yards for an early touchdown that gave the Volunteers a reason to believe.

There was Al Wilson, the jackhammer linebacker, jarring loose a fumble every time you turned around.

There was Tee Martin, the overwhelmed quarterback, mustering one brilliant touchdown pass to Peerless Price.

There was Deon Grant, the opportunistic safety, reaching up his hand and stealing away a Florida touchdown.

And after all this — after 60 minutes of sweat, tension, broken bodies and brilliant plays — the two teams were still tied at 17, and had settled nothing at all.

"It was a great battle," is how Fulmer would put it, later.

"Right past the end."

So Tennessee got the ball first. Tennessee gained one yard in three plays. Jeff Hall banged in a field goal of 41 yards.

But even then, you figured Florida would find a way to win, didn't you? A quick touchdown. An easy score. A typically emotionally crushing win.

But a funny thing happened on the way to consecutive win No. 6. The Tennessee defense dug in once again. The Florida quarterbacks fired three straight incompletions. Steve Spurrier waved in Cooper, going for the tie.

And the rest? Well you know the rest. The kick. The miss. The fans spilling onto the field.

So the goalposts fell. And the press box shook.

And good things had come to those who wait.

1929
Gene McEver..Halfback
1930
Bobby Dodd...Quarterback
1931
Herman Hickman ....Guard
1933
Beattie Feathers ....Halfback
1938
Bowden Wyatt...End
George Cafego...Halfback
Bob Suffridge ....Guard
1939
George Cafego...Halfback
Ed Molinski..Guard
Bob Suffridge ....Guard
Abe Shires ....Tackle
1940
Bob Suffridge ....Guard
Bob Foxx ....Halfback
Ed Molinski..Guard
1944
Bob Dobelstein ....Guard
1946
Dick Huffman ....Tackle
1950
Ted Daffer..Guard
Bud Sherrod...End
1951
Hank Lauricella ....Halfback
Ted Daffer..Guard
Bill Pearman..Tackle
1952
John Michels ....Guard
Doug Atkins ....Tackle
1954
Darris McCord..Tackle
1956
Johnny Majors..Halfback
Buddy Cruze ....End
1957
Bill Johnson...Guard
1963
Steve DeLong ....Guard
1964
Steve DeLong ....Guard
1965
Frank Emanuel ....Linebacker
1966
Paul Naumoff ....Linebacker
Austin Denny..End
Ron Widby ....Punter
Bob Johnson...Center
1967
Bob Johnson...Center
Albert Dorsey...Back
Richmond Flowers...Wingback

1968
Charles Rosenfelder..Guard
Steve Kiner ....Linebacker
Jim Weatherford..Back
1969
Steve Kiner ....Linebacker
Chip Kell...Guard
Jack Reynolds..Linebackers
1970
Chip Kell...Guard
Jackie Walker...Linebacker
1971
Bobby Majors..Back
Jackie Walker...Linebacker
1972
Conrad Graham..Back
Ricky Townsend ....Placekicker
Jamie Rotella..Linebacker
1973
Eddie Brown ....Back
Ricky Townsend ....Placekicker
1975
Larry Seivers ....Wide Receiver
1976
Larry Seivers ....Wide Receiver
1979
Roland James ....Back
1982
Willie Gault ....Wide Receiver
Jimmy Colquitt ....Punter
1983
Reggie White ....Tackle
Jimmy Colquitt ....Punter
1984
Bill Mayo ....Guard
1985
Tim McGee ....Wide Receiver
Chris White ....Defensive Back
1987
Harry Galbreath..Guard
1988
Keith DeLong...Linebacker
1989
Eric Still ....Guard
1990
Antone Davis ....Tackle
Dale Carter ....Defensive Back
1991
Dale Carter..Defensive Back
Carl Pickens ....Wide Receiver
1993
John Becksvoot ....Placekicker
1997
Peyton Manning ....Quarterback
Leonard Little..Linebacker

PHOTO CREDITS